E.T.A. Hoffmann

Titles in the series Critical Lives present the work of leading cultural figures of the modern period. Each book explores the life of the artist, writer, philosopher or architect in question and relates it to their major works.

In the same series

Hannah Arendt *Samantha Rose Hill*
Antonin Artaud *David A. Shafer*
John Ashbery *Jess Cotton*
Roland Barthes *Andy Stafford*
Georges Bataille *Stuart Kendall*
Charles Baudelaire *Rosemary Lloyd*
Jean Baudrillard *Emmanuelle Fantin and Bran Nicol*
Simone de Beauvoir *Ursula Tidd*
Samuel Beckett *Andrew Gibson*
Walter Benjamin *Esther Leslie*
John Berger *Andy Merrifield*
Leonard Bernstein *Paul R. Laird*
Joseph Beuys *Claudia Mesch*
Jorge Luis Borges *Jason Wilson*
Constantin Brancusi *Sanda Miller*
Bertolt Brecht *Philip Glahn*
Charles Bukowski *David Stephen Calonne*
Mikhail Bulgakov *J.A.E. Curtis*
William S. Burroughs *Phil Baker*
Byron *David Ellis*
John Cage *Rob Haskins*
Albert Camus *Edward J. Hughes*
Fidel Castro *Nick Caistor*
Paul Cézanne *Jon Kear*
Coco Chanel *Linda Simon*
Noam Chomsky *Wolfgang B. Sperlich*
Jean Cocteau *James S. Williams*
Joseph Conrad *Robert Hampson*
H.D. (Hilda Doolittle) *Lara Vetter*
Salvador Dalí *Mary Ann Caws*
Charles Darwin *J. David Archibald*
Guy Debord *Andy Merrifield*
Claude Debussy *David J. Code*
Gilles Deleuze *Frida Beckman*
Fyodor Dostoevsky *Robert Bird*
Marcel Duchamp *Caroline Cros*
Sergei Eisenstein *Mike O'Mahony*
Frantz Fanon *James S. Williams*
William Faulkner *Kirk Curnutt*
Gustave Flaubert *Anne Green*
Ford Madox Ford *Max Saunders*
Michel Foucault *David Macey*
Benjamin Franklin *Kevin J. Hayes*
Sigmund Freud *Matthew ffytche*
Mahatma Gandhi *Douglas Allen*
Antoni Gaudí *Michael Eaude*
Jean Genet *Stephen Barber*
Allen Ginsberg *Steve Finbow*
Johann Wolfgang von Goethe *Jeremy Adler*
Günter Grass *Julian Preece*
Ernest Hemingway *Verna Kale*
E.T.A. Hoffmann *Ritchie Robertson*
Langston Hughes *W. Jason Miller*
Victor Hugo *Bradley Stephens*
Zora Neale Hurston *Cheryl R. Hopson*
Aldous Huxley *Jake Poller*
J.-K. Huysmans *Ruth Antosh*
Christopher Isherwood *Jake Poller*
Derek Jarman *Michael Charlesworth*
Alfred Jarry *Jill Fell*
James Joyce *Andrew Gibson*
Carl Jung *Paul Bishop*
Franz Kafka *Sander L. Gilman*
Frida Kahlo *Gannit Ankori*
Søren Kierkegaard *Alastair Hannay*
Yves Klein *Nuit Banai*
Arthur Koestler *Edward Saunders*
Akira Kurosawa *Peter Wild*
D. H. Lawrence *David Ellis*
Lenin *Lars T. Lih*
Jack London *Kenneth K. Brandt*
Pierre Loti *Richard M. Berrong*
Rosa Luxemburg *Dana Mills*
Jean-François Lyotard *Kiff Bamford*
René Magritte *Patricia Allmer*
Gustav Mahler *Stephen Downes*
Stéphane Mallarmé *Roger Pearson*
Thomas Mann *Herbert Lehnert and Eva Wessell*
Gabriel García Márquez *Stephen M. Hart*
Karl Marx *Paul Thomas*
Henri Matisse *Kathryn Brown*
Guy de Maupassant *Christopher Lloyd*
Herman Melville *Kevin J. Hayes*
Henry Miller *David Stephen Calonne*
Yukio Mishima *Damian Flanagan*
Eadweard Muybridge *Marta Braun*
Vladimir Nabokov *Barbara Wyllie*
Pablo Neruda *Dominic Moran*
Friedrich Nietzsche *Ritchie Robertson*
Georgia O'Keeffe *Nancy J. Scott*
Richard Owen *Patrick Armstrong*
Octavio Paz *Nick Caistor*
Fernando Pessoa *Bartholomew Ryan*
Pablo Picasso *Mary Ann Caws*
Edgar Allan Poe *Kevin J. Hayes*
Ezra Pound *Alec Marsh*
Sergei Prokofiev *Christina Guillaumier*
Marcel Proust *Adam Watt*
Sergei Rachmaninoff *Rebecca Mitchell*
Maurice Ravel *Emily Kilpatrick*
Arthur Rimbaud *Seth Whidden*
John Ruskin *Andrew Ballantyne*
Jean-Paul Sartre *Andrew Leak*
Erik Satie *Mary E. Davis*
Arnold Schoenberg *Mark Berry*
Arthur Schopenhauer *Peter B. Lewis*
Dmitry Shostakovich *Pauline Fairclough*
Adam Smith *Jonathan Conlin*
Susan Sontag *Jerome Boyd Maunsell*
Gertrude Stein *Lucy Daniel*
Stendhal *Francesco Manzini*
Igor Stravinsky *Jonathan Cross*
Rabindranath Tagore *Bashabi Fraser*
Pyotr Tchaikovsky *Philip Ross Bullock*
Dylan Thomas *John Goodby and Chris Wigginton*
Leo Tolstoy *Andrei Zorin*
Leon Trotsky *Paul Le Blanc*
Mark Twain *Kevin J. Hayes*
Richard Wagner *Raymond Furness*
Alfred Russel Wallace *Patrick Armstrong*
Simone Weil *Palle Yourgrau*
Tennessee Williams *Paul Ibell*
Ludwig Wittgenstein *Edward Kanterian*
Virginia Woolf *Ira Nadel*
Frank Lloyd Wright *Robert McCarter*

E.T.A. Hoffmann

Ritchie Robertson

REAKTION BOOKS

To the memory of Siegbert Prawer (1925–2012), Hoffmann scholar and enthusiast

Published by Reaktion Books Ltd
2–4 Sebastian Street
London EC1V OHE, UK

www.reaktionbooks.co.uk

First published 2025

EU GPSR Authorised Representative
Logos Europe, 9 rue Nicolas Poussin, 17000, La Rochelle, France
email: contact@logoseurope.eu

Printed and bound in Great Britain by Bell & Bain, Glasgow

A catalogue record for this book is available from the British Library

ISBN 978 1 83639 101 2

Contents

Abbreviations and Citations

The list of abbreviations includes the editions I have cited; I have referred to English translations where possible and to Hartmut Steinecke's edition in the many cases where translations are not available. Where no translator is specified, translations are my own. Quotations in the text are identified as economically as possible by references to these editions, with volume and page number where appropriate: for example, H II/2, 129 indicates Hoffmann's *Sämtliche Werke* (as detailed below), volume II, book 2, p. 129. Letters are identified by date only, which is sufficient to find them in the *Sämtliche Werke*.

A — *E.T.A. Hoffmann in Aufzeichnungen seiner Freunde und Bekannten*, ed. Friedrich Schnapp (Munich, 1974)

AMZ — *Allgemeine musikalische Zeitung*

C — *E.T.A. Hoffmann's Musical Writings*, ed. David Charlton and trans. Martyn Clarke (Cambridge, 1989)

DE — E.T.A. Hoffmann, *The Devil's Elixirs*, trans. Ronald Taylor (London, 1963)

GP — E.T.A. Hoffmann, *The Golden Pot and Other Tales*, trans. Ritchie Robertson (Oxford, 1992)

H — E.T.A. Hoffmann, *Sämtliche Werke*, 6 vols (in 7 books), ed. Hartmut Steinecke et al. (Frankfurt, 1985–2003)

MHG — *Mitteilungen der E.T.A. Hoffmann-Gesellschaft*

Murr — E.T.A. Hoffmann, *The Life and Opinions of the Tomcat Murr*, trans. Anthea Bell (London, 1999)

Tales — *Tales of Hoffmann*, trans. R. J. Hollingdale et al. (Harmondsworth, 1982)

Introduction

Of all the German writers conventionally classed as Romantics, Ernst Theodor Amadeus Hoffmann (1776–1822) has the widest international reputation. His literary works are in prose, which is relatively easy to translate, whereas the riches of Romantic poetry are accessible only to those who can read them in the original. Hoffmann has attracted distinguished translators, beginning with Thomas Carlyle and R. P. Gillies in the 1820s, and, in recent decades, R. J. Hollingdale, Ronald Taylor, Anthea Bell and Jack Zipes.

Many readers, however, form their first impression of Hoffmann from Jacques Offenbach's opera *Les Contes d'Hoffmann* (The Tales of Hoffmann, 1881), with a libretto by Jules Barbier and Michel Carré. Here a convivial Hoffmann, drinking in a tavern, becomes the protagonist of supernatural adventures based on three of his tales. This Hoffmann is an arch-Romantic figure, inspired by the interplay of intoxication and imagination, and the victim of dark forces. Mixing biography and fiction, Barbier and Carré provide, at the very best, an image of Hoffmann so one-sided as to be highly misleading.

Hoffmann was not only a prolific author but a composer, caricaturist, music reviewer and the writer of searching essays on aesthetics. He was also an outstanding lawyer whose judgements are still rewarding to read. The precision of his legal writings informs his stories: though often written in a headlong style, heavy with evocative adjectives, they are not mere rhapsodies but carefully and intricately conceived masterpieces that survive minute analysis. Often, especially in his Gothic narratives, Hoffmann denies the reader any obvious explanation and leaves his tales open to multiple interpretations. This sense of ever-receding, ultimately unfathomable depths is essential to his art, and is conveyed also in his reflections on music, though here metaphors of height, loftiness and sublimity rather than depth are appropriate.

In this biography, while inevitably going into detail about Hoffmann's fiction, I have acknowledged his achievements in other fields, notably his opera *Undine* (1816). His work in various media cannot easily be aligned with phases of his life, which in any case was repeatedly disrupted by the Napoleonic Wars. For a long time, Hoffmann hoped to make a career in music, but a series of setbacks obliged him to fall back on his legal training. Although he rose to become a senior judge in Berlin, he had by then established such a literary reputation that he was under constant pressure from publishers and magazine editors to supply them with stories. That explains the sheer quantity of his fiction, which has required me to be severely selective in the works I discuss. Not all Hoffmann's fictional works are masterpieces, but none of them are dull. Add to this that Hoffmann, though not the drunkard presented by Offenbach, was highly convivial and loved to spend evenings in a wine cellar near his Berlin flat. It is perhaps no wonder that he died, burned out, in 1822 at the age of 46.

1

From Königsberg to Berlin, from Music to Literature

The Romantic writer known to posterity as Ernst Theodor Amadeus Hoffmann was actually christened Ernst Theodor Wilhelm, and continued to use that name throughout his life for official purposes. His adopting the name Amadeus around 1804 may be seen not only as a homage to Wolfgang Amadeus Mozart but as an affirmation of his identity as an artist. Though his most substantial achievement by far was in literary fiction, he thought of himself primarily as a composer. However, a musical career was eventually made impossible by the difficult circumstances of his life, which obliged him reluctantly to resume the legal career for which he had been trained.

These difficulties began in childhood. Ernst's parents, Christoph Ludwig Hoffmann (1736–1797), an improvident and hard-drinking lawyer, and the rigidly respectable and status-conscious Luise Albertina, née Doerffer (1748–1796), who came from a long-established family in the north German city of Königsberg, divorced when he was two years old. Divorce, including no-fault divorce, was relatively easy under Prussian law, but it still carried a stigma. In 1782 Christoph moved to a legal post in the nearby town of Insterburg, taking with him only his elder son Karl. Christoph died fifteen years later after suffering two strokes. Karl, who seems to have inherited his father's worst qualities, played little part in Ernst's life. Receiving an unwelcome visit from Karl in 1796, Ernst complained in a letter that his brother was frivolous and untrustworthy (H I, 60), and his only surviving letter to his brother, in 1817 (drafted, but not sent), is apparently in response to a request for money (H VI, 120–22).[1]

Luise Hoffmann returned to her mother's house in a prosperous quarter of Königsberg, where Ernst was brought up. For someone who would grow into a great humorous writer, the setting was unpropitious. His grandmother, though the dominant member of the family, was frail and largely housebound. She shared the house with her four adult children. Luise, demoralized by divorce, became depressed and seldom left her room. Her brother Otto (1741–1811), a lawyer who had retired early because of professional failure, spent his abundant leisure in obsessively orderly routines. Ernst's two aunts treated the boy kindly; the younger, Charlotte, died of smallpox when he was three, but her sister Johanna, who lived until 1803, gave the boy sympathy and understanding.

The family were musical. His father played the viola da gamba, his aunt Charlotte the lute, his uncle Otto the piano and, if we can trust the semi-autobiographical recollections that Hoffmann later put in the mouth of his fictional alter ego Kreisler, the child also experienced the spinet (a small harpsichord) and the trumpet marine.[2] Uncle Otto taught Ernst the piano, so that as a boy he soon astonished his elders by revealing a talent for musical improvisation. His uncle also instilled in him a respect for systematic study and a habit of disciplined work, which would later benefit Hoffmann both as an artist and as a lawyer.

For some time, the top floor of the house was tenanted by a widow, Frau Werner, whose mental health was poor and who was frequently heard moaning. She believed that she was destined to give birth to the saviour of the world. Her actual son, Zacharias (1768–1823), did in fact become the outstanding German Romantic dramatist. Although they had little contact in Königsberg, Zacharias being five years older, in adult life he and Hoffmann had a fraught relationship; Hoffmann described him in print as 'selfish, egoistic, disloyal to friends' (H II/1, 175).

'In my early upbringing, left to myself between four walls, lie the seeds of many follies committed subsequently,' Hoffmann recalled in 1803 (H I, 134). Without a father, and living with a depressed and distant mother, his childhood has been interpreted as traumatic, and it has been plausibly argued that some of his finest fiction addresses his traumas by pitting a child's perspective against an authoritarian and loveless adult world.[3] Fortunately the loneliness of his childhood was alleviated by a school friend, Theodor Gottlieb Hippel (1775–1843), an only child, who was allowed to visit him, ostensibly to help with homework, on Wednesdays and Saturdays. The two boys spent much time on books (including Rousseau's *Confessions*), music, games, dressing up, and such exploits as trying to dig a tunnel in order to look at the young ladies in the boarding school next door (Uncle Otto nipped this in the bud). Hippel's uncle, also called Theodor Gottlieb (1741–1796), a respected citizen who became mayor of Königsberg, published humorous novels, a treatise on marriage and a plea for women's emancipation (*On the Civil Improvement of Women*, 1792), all anonymously. Hoffmann's letters to Hippel junior, along with Hippel's recollections published after Hoffmann's death, are the main source for knowledge of Hoffmann's early years.

By the turn of the nineteenth century, Königsberg was a thriving commercial city with about 50,000 inhabitants, a vigorous musical life and of course a university, whose academic star was Immanuel Kant (1724–1804). Nowadays the city is called Kaliningrad, so named after a Bolshevik leader, and is the capital of a Russian exclave, separated by Poland and Lithuania from Russia's main territory. As an ice-free port it was too important for Russia to sacrifice. In the Second World War the city was severely damaged by British bombing, and after the war the German population was expelled as part of Soviet ethnic cleansing. Today, many buildings have been restored, including the cathedral, and an E.T.A. Hoffmann museum has been founded. In the story 'Das Majorat' ('The Entail', 1817), the bleak Baltic coast is evoked with the atmosphere of Gothic fiction in one of Hoffmann's few landscape descriptions:

> Not far from the shore of the Baltic there stands Castle R., the ancestral seat of Baron von R. The district is wild and desolate; hardly anything grows, a blade of grass here and there in the bottomless quicksand; and, instead of a castle garden, a scanty pine-forest cleaves to the bare walls on the landward side – a place

> of external gloom in which there echoes only the croaking of ravens and the screams of storm-proclaiming seagulls. (*Tales* 185)

The British reader who wants to imagine Hoffmann's home region more soberly may do well to think of Aberdeen – a commercial city, remote from other centres of population, on a rocky coast, with an ancient university.

Hoffmann and Hippel both studied law. It does not appear that Hoffmann took any interest in Kant: he was probably not among the third of the student body who attended Kant's lectures (and who did so despite the great man's notoriously soporific delivery). In 1800 he spent a convivial evening with an English merchant named Lewison, who had lived in Königsberg and could imitate Kant (H I, 129). As a student Hoffmann often gave private music lessons; he would continue doing this over many years to supplement his often meagre income. Occasionally Hoffmann was able to extend his experience by accompanying his uncle, Christoph Ernst Voeteri (1722–1795), a semi-retired lawyer, to various landed estates; this provided material that Hoffmann later exploited in 'The Entail'. Hoffmann completed his undergraduate studies in 1795 and became

Unknown artist, *The Green Bridge with the New Stock Exchange and Stores in Königsberg*, *c*. 1810, watercolour drawing.

a trainee observer (*Auskultator*) at the high court in Königsberg. Thereafter he had to pass three professional examinations, which he achieved with excellent grades, the last in 1800.

Hippel meanwhile obtained a post in the Prussian town of Marienwerder. Although carried on largely by letter, and impeded by Hoffmann's slackness in writing (the 'Brieffaulheit' of which he accused himself, H I, 150), this was the most important friendship of the first thirty years of Hoffmann's life. Hoffmann often writes in the high-flown emotional style common in the age of sensibility, as in his letters of 28 February 1795 – 'You are the only one who understands the inner stirrings of my heart' – and 25 January 1803: 'If you feel as intensely as I do that we can never, never cease to love each other, then I am very happy!' Hoffmann's letters give a strong impression of emotional neediness. In the latter quotation, he seems to be overcompensating for the gradual cooling of their friendship. In 1797 Hippel inherited an estate, so no longer needed to earn a living, and married a young woman of fifteen. On a journey that year, Hoffmann stopped at the mansion of Hippel's prospective in-laws and spoke to Hippel for ten minutes on the steps amid wind and rain; after what Hoffmann later called 'our romantic meeting' in a letter of 10 May 1797, they saw each other only rarely until a chance meeting in Dresden in 1813.

All this time Hoffmann was developing his lifelong devotion to music. From his uncle's early lessons, he passed to professional teachers, notably Christian Podbielski, organist of Königsberg Cathedral; later on, Hoffmann would portray Podbielski affectionately as 'Master Abraham' in *Lebens-Ansichten des Katers Murr* (The Life and Opinions of the Tomcat Murr, 1819–21). When living in Berlin in 1798–1800, he took lessons from Johann Friedrich Reichardt, a native of Königsberg who became musical director at the Prussian court in 1776 but whose career was damaged because of his sympathetic stance on the French Revolution. Königsberg was a musical town, with many public and private concerts. Operettas or *Singspiele* (comedies with simple plots, spoken dialogue and frequent songs) enjoyed great popularity, but the public could also appreciate serious operas: in 1793 Mozart's *Don Giovanni* was performed six times, and the following year there was great enthusiasm for *The Magic Flute*.[4] Early in 1795 Hoffmann spent several weeks studying the music of *Don Giovanni* in a version for the piano, discovering ever more nuances in 'this unique music' (4 March 1795); it became his favourite opera. He himself sang (he was a tenor) and played the piano, violin and harp.

In addition, Hoffmann drew, painted, read and wrote. 'During the week I'm a lawyer and, at most, a bit of a musician; on Sundays I draw during the day and in the evening I'm a very witty author until late at night' (23 January 1796). In his first surviving letter, dated October 1794, he tells how he offered two paintings anonymously to Hippel's uncle, the mayor of Königsberg; the mayor liked the paintings and wished to meet the artist, but when the pair met, Hoffmann discovered that the mayor thought the paintings were intended as a present, and of course could hardly correct him.

Hoffmann's favourite writer seems to have been Shakespeare, judging from the frequency with which both he and his fictional characters quote from the plays (especially *Twelfth Night*, *Henry IV* and *Hamlet*). He also read Friedrich Schiller (1759–1805) and compared his friendship with Hippel to the high-flown, sentimental friendship between Carlos and Posa in *Don Carlos*; later he produced a humorously macabre story based on *Die Räuber* (The Robbers), in which two travellers, staying at a castle, realize that their hosts are the tragic family of Schiller's play (H V, 709–54). In particular, Hoffmann read the great humorists: Laurence Sterne (1713–1768), whose sentimental style is often echoed in letters to Hippel; Jean Paul (Johann Paul Friedrich Richter, 1763–1825), Sterne's German counterpart, at that time hugely popular; François Rabelais (d. 1553); and Miguel de Cervantes (1547–1616). Given his later reputation, it is not surprising to find him reporting in his letter of 19 February 1795 that he is immersed in Carl Grosse's elaborate horror story *Der Genius* (The Genius; also popular in Britain under the title *Horrid Mysteries*), published from 1791 to 1795. Later he would devour the classic tales of terror, Schiller's *Der Geisterseher* (The Ghost-Seer, 1787–9) and M. G. Lewis's *The Monk* (1796).[5] In the 1790s he wrote two novels in this genre, *Cornaro* and

The Mysterious Man, and hoped to get them published, but neither survives (A 34–5).

Hoffmann still earned money by giving music lessons. One of his pupils was Dorothea ('Dora') Hatt (1766–1803), ten years his senior, the wife of a well-to-do cloth merchant and, when Hoffmann first became enamoured of her, mother of five children. How serious his feelings were may be questioned. He wrote to Hippel: 'I doubt very much whether I love my inamorata with all the emotion of which my heart would be capable' (12 December 1794). Perhaps he was cultivating a passion for Dora in order to fill an emotional void. Later, in 1804, Hoffmann received a visit from Dora's daughter Amalie ('Malchen'), who informed him of her mother's death: Hoffmann's diary records 'a sweet unknown melancholy' and the strong impression made by Malchen's beauty (13 February 1804, H I, 247).

At the time, Hoffmann's feelings for Dora were powerful enough to bring about a public confrontation with her husband at a masked ball in January 1796. We do not know exactly what happened, for Hippel, before handing over Hoffmann's letters to his first biographer, erased the relevant passage, but a later letter mentions a 'bull scene', implying that Hoffmann and Hatt confronted each other like two enraged bulls (22 February 1796).

After this public scandal, Hoffmann's relatives decided that he must leave Königsberg. They sent him to live under the supervision of an uncle, Johann Ludwig Doerffer (1743–1803), in Glogau, a town in the Prussian province of Silesia with a largely Polish population (now Głogów in Poland). The Doerffers were a cultivated family; his aunt is said to have been a first-rate singer (A 43). While working in Glogau he met a painter, Aloys Molinary (1772–1831), and helped him to paint the Jesuit church; Molinary was a handsome, imposing figure who conveyed 'a certain superiority that was never presumptuous' (22 January 1797), and inspired the figure of Berthold, the doom-laden painter in 'Die Jesuiterkirche in G–' ('The Jesuit Church in G[logau], 1817).

Hoffmann's progress over the next few years, which were largely uncreative, can be recounted briefly. In 1798 he was able to move to a junior post in Berlin, and after passing his final professional exam in 1800 he was appointed as *Assessor* (assistant judge) at the high court in Posen (now Poznań), in Prussian-occupied Poland. There, however, he damaged his career by drawing caricatures of Posen notables, which were offered for sale by masked figures at carnival parties in February 1802. As punishment he was transferred to Płock, a tiny town of 3,000 inhabitants, a cultural desert, where he felt 'buried alive' (25 January 1803). Through good behaviour and by demonstrating his outstanding legal abilities, he managed in 1804 to get himself transferred to Warsaw, a city of some 70,000 inhabitants, which at first felt noisy and confusing after the provincial monotony of Płock, but which offered enormous cultural variety and stimulus.

Meanwhile, Hoffmann's private life was developing after the Dora Hatt affair. In 1798 he became engaged to his cousin Minna (Sophie Wilhelmine Konstantine Doerffer, 1775–after 1832), the daughter of the uncle with whom he was living in Glogau. There was nothing romantic about this attachment. Getting married was vital to a professional career, and Minna was already familiar to Hoffmann. However, he was in no hurry to marry Minna, and the engagement dragged on until his disgrace in Posen made the Doerffers consider him ineligible as a husband. Before leaving Posen, however, he met and married Marianna Thekla Michalina Rorer (1778–1859), daughter of the town clerk, and she accompanied him into exile.

Mischa, as Hoffmann called her, is a somewhat shadowy figure. No image of her exists. In a long letter to Hippel written in the spring of 1803, Hoffmann described her in strikingly external terms: '22 years old, moderate height – good figure, dark brown hair, dark blue eyes, etc.' (H I, 136). Her German was imperfect: Hoffmann wrote on 28 April 1812 of how amusing it was to hear her say the word *Landleute* (country folk) when she meant *Landsleute* (fellow countrymen). No other spoken or written utterance by Mischa survives except for one: when the theatre next door burned down in 1817, she exclaimed, 'My God, the theatre's on fire!' (15 December). His friends report that Mischa was modest, undemanding, good-humoured and patient with Hoffmann's mood swings.

He always referred to her affectionately, but given Hoffmann's varied professional, artistic and convivial activities they cannot have spent much time together. The couple looked after Mischa's niece Michalina (b. 1795) until her marriage in 1813. They had a daughter of their own, Cäcilia, who died in August 1807 at the age of two. The child's death may have created an emotional distance between them, but what one says about Mischa can hardly be more than conjecture.

Musical Activity in Warsaw

In contrast to Berlin or Königsberg, Warsaw was a multicultural city. Besides the majority Polish population, Turks, Greeks, Russians and Jews were also conspicuous in the bustling urban landscape. There were German and Polish theatres, a troupe of French actors and an Italian opera house. This description comes from Hoffmann's colleague Julius Eduard Hitzig (1780–1849), who arrived there from Berlin as an *Assessor* in 1804, formed a lasting friendship with him and would later be his executor and first biographer. Hitzig, born Isaac Elias Itzig, belonged to a prominent Berlin Jewish family of bankers and businessmen; the Itzigs were related to the Mendelssohns, whose best-known member was the Enlightenment philosopher Moses Mendelssohn (1729–1786) – one of Hitzig's aunts was the mother of the composer Felix Mendelssohn-Bartholdy (1809–1847). Hitzig had many friends and contacts in Berlin literary circles: he frequented the salon of the Jewish hostess Rahel Varnhagen (1771–1833) and knew such Romantic writers and thinkers as the poet Clemens Brentano (1778–1842), the storyteller and traveller Adelbert von Chamisso (1781–1838) and the theologian Friedrich Schleiermacher (1768–1834). Thanks to Hitzig, Hoffmann learned about Romanticism as a literary movement. Hitzig introduced him to the poetry and prose of Novalis (Friedrich von Hardenberg, 1772–1801) – whose early death combined with his exceptional gifts gave him a saintly status resembling that of Keats in Britain – and to one of the key works of early Romanticism, the novel *Franz Sternbalds Wanderungen* (The Wanderings of Franz Sternbald) by Ludwig Tieck (1773–1853), about a painter travelling to Italy to fulfil his vocation. Hoffmann in turn urged Hippel to read Tieck's novel, which he called 'this true artist's book' (26 September 1805).[6]

Music, however, was Hoffmann's first love, though it brought him many frustrations. Over eighteen years, according to a leading Hoffmann scholar, he composed eight operas and *Singspiele*, twenty-three pieces of stage music, several Masses, one *Miserere* (setting of Psalm 51), a symphony, some thirty songs and choruses, and fifteen pieces of piano or chamber music.[7] Many of these are lost. Hoffmann managed to publish only a handful: a piano sonata (in a Polish journal), three canzonettas, six Italian duettinos and a piano composition (which, though published, cannot now be traced). His first substantial surviving piece dates from 1799, his first Berlin period: it is a *Singspiel* entitled *Die Maske* (The Mask), of which Hoffmann wrote the text as well as the score. Both were lost until their rediscovery by Friedrich Schnapp in 1921. The action, as usual in a *Singspiel*, is flimsy and formulaic, turning on lovers being separated and reunited, and long-lost relatives being recognized. Hoffmann sent the text to August Wilhelm Iffland, director of the Königliches Nationaltheater in Berlin, but Iffland rejected it and did not even bother to ask for the score. The work has been praised in recent years for skilfully integrating music with the dramatic flow of the text in the manner pioneered by Mozart in *Die Entführung aus dem Serail* (The Abduction from the Seraglio, 1782).[8]

During his dispiriting years in Posen and Płock, Hoffmann at least continued composing. The first of his works to be performed in public, a cantata celebrating the new century, was performed in Posen on 31 December 1800. He composed music for a *Singspiel* by Goethe entitled *Scherz, List und Rache* (Jest, Cunning and Revenge), which was performed several times in autumn 1801; the score has since been lost. In Płock, Hoffmann tried unsuccessfully to get his compositions published. He sent a Fantasia in C minor to the music publisher Nägeli in Zurich, and a piano sonata to Schott in Mainz, but neither was accepted. He entered a literary competition with a comedy, *Der Preis* (The Prize), whose subject was the competition itself. Despite being unsuccessful, it was commended by the judges, who said that of all the contestants Hoffmann showed the greatest potential as an author of comedies. Although *Der Preis* is lost, this judgement can be supported by the fragmentary opera *Der Renegat* (The Renegade), written in 1804. It belongs to the popular genre of *Türkenopern* (operas featuring Christian captives in Muslim countries), whose best-known example is Mozart's *Die Entführung*. Hoffmann's libretto features a humorous contrast between the pathos of the nobleman St Cyr and the down-to-earth common sense of his servant Joseph. The action is amusing and ingenious: St Cyr has come in quest of his lover Elisa, who has been kidnapped and taken to Algiers by a corsair, who is in fact a French convert to Islam (hence a renegade); unfortunately, the opera breaks off after only five scenes. In correspondence from 11 to 14 May 1804, Hoffmann told Hippel that because of his burdensome legal work, the opera would probably not be finished until 1888.

The move to Warsaw reanimated Hoffmann's musical ambitions. During his time there (1804–7) he composed a great deal and was energetic in organizing the Ressource Musical Society, which put on amateur concerts. Hoffmann was its vice-president and in charge of its musical library. When the Ressource acquired as premises the unoccupied and dilapidated Mniszech Palace, Hoffmann supervised the interior decoration and painted the walls himself, and arranged for the society to buy an Erard grand piano, which was ordered from Paris. At the society's opening concert, on 3 August 1806, Hoffmann made his first appearance as a conductor, presenting his Symphony in E-flat. Hitzig reports that the audience admired 'his calm and measured behaviour, despite his quicksilver restlessness . . . His *tempi* were fiery and fast, without any exaggeration' (A 107, 110). For the society Hoffmann also wrote his Quintet for harp, two violins, viola and cello, besides a piano quintet in D (which is lost). He also gave solo performances as a singer.

One of Hoffmann's first musical projects was to set to music a *Singspiel* entitled *Die lustigen Musikanten* (The Merry Musicians) by Clemens Brentano. He valued this work so highly that, whereas his previous compositions had been anonymous, he signed it, using for the first time the name 'Amadeus' instead of 'Wilhelm'. It was completed in December 1804 and performed on 6 April 1805.

The music scholar Gerhard Allroggen not only considers it the outstanding musical comedy of early nineteenth-century Germany but praises its originality (H II/2, 726); a more recent authority, John Warrack, agrees, finding in it 'much original invention, making some use of a rising and falling chromatic scale as a motivic idea'.[9] It conforms to the popular eighteenth-century type of the 'number opera', in which self-contained arias, duets or tercets are linked by spoken dialogue or recitatives, but in at least one scene individual numbers are replaced with ensembles and recitatives, thus moving towards the integrated or *durchkomponiert* (through-composed) opera that would later culminate in Richard Wagner's concept of 'endless melody'. The piece's performance, however, was hampered by the incompetence of the singers. Nevertheless, it received a review – deploring the performers but praising the composition – in the widely read periodical *Zeitung für die elegante Welt*, based in Leipzig.

The author of the review was Hoffmann's long-standing acquaintance Zacharias Werner, now also a civil servant in Warsaw, who proved that his praise was sincere by asking Hoffmann to supply incidental music for his play *Das Kreuz an der Ostsee* (The Cross on the Baltic, 1805), a spectacular drama concerning the advent of Christianity among the heathen Prussians. Much later, Hoffmann told an anecdote about a reading of the play. When the curtain rises, the Prussians are supposed to be collecting amber on the shore of the Baltic and invoking their goddess. Werner, 'pulling one of his extraordinary, indescribable faces', began: 'Bankputtis! – Bankputtis! – Bankputtis!', whereupon somebody piped up and asked whether the whole play was composed in this language, and, if so, whether Werner could provide a translation (H IV, 1028) – the questioner was actually Hoffmann (A 94). Hoffmann found Werner to be a trial to work with: he was insufferably anxious, always pestering the composer to meet tight deadlines. The play, with Hoffmann's score, was offered to the Königliches Nationaltheater but Iffland rejected it on the grounds that it was too 'colossal' to be stageable – yet another disappointment for Hoffmann.[10]

Undeterred, Hoffmann persevered with ambitious projects, notably the music for a play by the seventeenth-century Spanish

Friedrich August Calau, *The Berlin Schauspielhaus in 1817*, before 1839, aquatint.

dramatist Pedro Calderón de la Barca (1600–1681). Calderón was intensely admired by the German Romantics and also by Goethe.[11] The critic August Wilhelm Schlegel (1767–1845) translated several of his plays into German, including *La devoción de la Cruz* (The Devotion of the Cross), which was a favourite of the Romantics, and the comedy *La banda y la flor* (The Sash and the Flower). The latter so appealed to Hoffmann that he adapted it as an opera, changing the title to *Liebe und Eifersucht* (Love and Jealousy), writing both text and music. He had great hopes for it, telling Hitzig in April 1807 that 'it will leave all my other compositions far behind.' Like so many of Hoffmann's musical works, however, it was never performed.

Hoffmann's musical achievement, apart from his masterly opera *Undine*, is difficult to assess, especially as so many of his works are lost. For most of the nineteenth century his musical works were forgotten. Only in the early twentieth century did they come into some focus. Even then, it was common to disparage the musician Hoffmann as a dilettante whose real interest was in literature, or to pigeonhole him as an imitator of Mozart. Ronald Taylor, who was a music historian as well as a professor of German studies, found Hoffmann's compositions technically competent but 'pedestrian', though he acknowledged 'flashes of a Mozartian idiom' in *Undine*.[12] Allroggen has defended Hoffmann against both these charges, pointing out that he always regarded music as his vocation, while literature was, at best, a second string.[13] Allroggen concludes, nevertheless, that because of the pressures of his professional employment and his need to supplement his income by writing fiction, Hoffmann did not manage to fulfil his potential as a composer.

Hoffmann's place in musical history is somewhat surprising. It is often remarked that he does not fit the image of the Romantic composer. His works are relatively sedate, whereas from the creator of the musician alter ego Kreisler we might have expected stormy music anticipating Robert Schumann (1810–1856).[14] Hoffmann's music is rooted in earlier traditions. One, to which his teachers Podbielski and Reichardt belonged, is the north German tradition centring on Johann Sebastian Bach (1685–1750).[15] Kreisler is a devotee of Bach's Goldberg Variations, which around 1800 were thought too difficult to be appreciated, and insists on playing them to torment his uncomprehending hearers (C 84–5). Another tradition is that of church music, going back to the sixteenth-century Renaissance composer Palestrina, to which Hoffmann pays ample tribute in 'Alte und neue Kirchenmusik' ('Old and New Church Music', 1814), discussed later. He had a baroque taste for musical-verbal jokes, as when, in his setting of Werner's *Cross on the Baltic*, a drinking song in honour of the god Pikollos uses the piccolo.[16] His north German severity was softened by familiarity with Gluck, Haydn and Mozart, though he deplored the 'ostentatious frivolity' to which he found Viennese composers inclined.[17] Mozart's influence, alongside that of Italian church music, has been detected especially in his *Miserere*, and his only symphony has been described as closely indebted to Mozart's Symphony No. 39 in E-flat major.[18] Finally, Hoffmann the composer would himself become influential. Wagner, who admired *Undine*, noticed its use of 'recurring themes to identify characters and situations', and developed this into the technique of the leitmotif.[19] The many echoes that have been identified in Hoffmann's work do not make him a minor or merely derivative composer: they suggest, first, his position in a transitional phase of music history;

second, his eclectic tastes; and third, his skill at composing works that, however diverse their impulses, were – as a sensitive tribute marking the centenary of his death emphasized – always unified and 'durchkomponiert'.[20] *Undine* and its relation to the Romantic opera typified by Carl Maria von Weber's *Der Freischütz* (The Freeshooter, 1821) will be considered later.

Hoffmann as Music Critic

However he may be ranked as a composer, Hoffmann was an outstanding music critic, particularly of Beethoven. In 1809 Hoffmann sent the short story 'Ritter Gluck' ('The Chevalier Gluck') to Friedrich Rochlitz, editor of the Leipzig-based *Allgemeine musikalische Zeitung* (*AMZ*), adding that he was willing to write reviews. Rochlitz accepted the story, commissioned two reviews and asked Hoffmann particularly to review works by Beethoven. Hoffmann thus became the lead reviewer for the foremost musical periodical in the German-speaking world. From 1809 to 1815 he wrote a large number of reviews, based on scores, including five works by Beethoven, the opera *Sofonisba* by Ferdinando Paer (C 263–70), the First Symphony by Louis Spohr (C 272–86), a piano score of Christoph Willibald Gluck's *Iphigénie en Aulide* (C 256–62), and much more. The standard pattern of reviews in the *AMZ* was an introduction followed by extensive technical analysis and a conclusion. Hoffmann followed this pattern but developed it by using the introduction to evoke the effect of the music.[21] Thus in his review of Beethoven's *Coriolan* overture, his opening paragraph reflected on Beethoven's 'romantic genius' and how it seemed at odds with the 'predominantly reflective poetry' of the drama *Coriolan* by Heinrich von Collin (1771–1811). Hence: 'The sombre gravity of the present composition, with its awe-inspiring resonances from an unknown spirit-world, foreshadows more than is subsequently fulfilled' (C 287).

The single most important review by Hoffmann deals with Beethoven's Fifth Symphony. He adapted some passages from this as well as his review of Beethoven's piano trios Op. 70 (nos 1 and 2) for his essay 'Beethovens Instrumental-Musik' ('Beethoven's Instrumental Music'), included in his first book publication, *Fantasiestücke in Callots Manier* (Fantasy-Pieces in the Manner of Callot, 1814–15). This essay forms an epoch-making statement, not only of Hoffmann's musical aesthetics but of the principles of Romanticism (though Hoffmann's use of the term 'romantic' is somewhat idiosyncratic), and deserves detailed quotation and discussion. The essay begins:

> When music is spoken of as an independent art, does not the term properly apply only to instrumental music, which scorns all aid, all admixture of other arts (poetry), and gives pure expression to its own peculiar artistic nature? It is the most romantic of all arts, one might almost say the only one that is genuinely romantic, since its only subject-matter is infinity. Orpheus' lyre opened the gates of Orcus. Music reveals to man an unknown realm, a world quite separate from the outer sensual world surrounding him, a world in which he leaves behind all precise feelings in order to embrace an inexpressible longing. (C 96)

Only a few composers are able to unlock 'the wonderful realm of the romantic' (C 98). They include Haydn, Mozart and Beethoven. The first two are 'the creators of modern instrumental music' (C 97), but Beethoven is 'the one who regarded it with total devotion and penetrated to its innermost nature' (C 97).

Haydn romantically apprehends the humanity in everyday life; he is more congenial, more comprehensible to the majority. Mozart takes more as his province the superhuman, magical quality residing in the human self ('im innern Geiste', H II/1, 54). Beethoven's music sets in motion the machinery of awe, of fear, of terror, of pain, and awakens 'that infinite yearning which is the essence of romanticism'. He is therefore a purely romantic composer (C 98).

What did Hoffmann mean by 'romantic' here? He is drawing on the aesthetics of early German Romanticism, formulated by Friedrich Schlegel in his essays in the journal *Athenäum* and by Ludwig Tieck and Wilhelm Wackenroder in their rhapsodic *Herzensergießungen eines kunstliebenden Klosterbruders* (Effusions of an Art-Loving Monk, 1797). Tieck and Wackenroder have their monk say:

> The artist must first encounter every beautiful work within himself, but must not labour to seek himself in it; art must be his higher beloved, for it is of heavenly origin and must be precious to him, second only to religion; it must become a religious love or a beloved religion.[22]

The religion of art, proclaimed in this influential Romantic manifesto, readily turned into art as religion, and we shall see presently how far Hoffmann's aesthetics followed the same path.

In his use of the word 'romantic', Hoffmann is not drawing the now familiar contrast of romanticism and classicism. Rather, 'romantic' denotes the interplay between the composer's creative methods and the listener's (including the performer's) powers of musical appreciation. Hoffmann disputes the common opinion that Beethoven is a disorderly, unmethodical genius who 'dashes everything down just as the feverish workings of his imagination dictate to him at that moment' (C 98). Far from it, Hoffmann contends. Beethoven's essential quality is *Besonnenheit*, or 'rational awareness' (C 98; H II/1, 54). He knows exactly what he is doing: 'In truth, he is fully the equal of Haydn and Mozart in rational awareness, his controlling self detached from the inner realm of sounds and ruling it in absolute authority' (C 98). Such music demands a responsive audience. As Hoffmann says elsewhere, 'Only a romantic and profound spirit can fully appreciate the romantic and profound Mozart' (C 261). Beethoven's music does not offer gratuitous displays of technical virtuosity. It has a 'gravity' that 'rules out all the breakneck passages up and down the keyboard with both hands, all the odd leaps, the whimsical flourishes . . . with which the most recent piano compositions are replete' (C 102).

> The proper performance of Beethoven's works demands nothing less than that one understands him, that one penetrates to his

inner nature, and that in the knowledge of one's own state of grace [*Weihe*] one ventures boldly into the circle of magical beings that his irresistible spell summons forth. (C 103)

Although this essay elicited a letter of thanks from Beethoven (C 62), its importance extends far beyond the individual composer. It is a landmark in music history because it makes a decisive case for instrumental music, independent of words (in songs, librettos and so on), as the supreme form of music, and hence the supreme form of art. In the eighteenth century, music, like other arts, was considered a form of imitation. The French encyclopaedist Jean Le Rond d'Alembert (1717–1783) said that music imitates agreeable or disagreeable sounds and thereby arouses the appropriate emotions.[23] Kant ranked music lowest among the fine arts on the grounds that it 'merely plays with sensations' and has no rational content.[24] Hoffmann, by contrast, puts forward an expressive aesthetic. Music communicates something that cannot be conveyed in any other medium: the yearning for a spiritual realm, which is quintessentially romantic.

Hoffmann's aesthetics apply even beyond music. The 'rational awareness' that Hoffmann attributes to Beethoven is, for him, a feature of the greatest art. In the long and important dialogue on drama *Seltsame Leiden eines Theater-Direktors* (Strange Sufferings of a Theatre Director), published in book form in 1819, Hoffmann ascribes it to Shakespeare, quoting the aesthetician Carl Ludwig Fernow (1763–1808), who credits the English playwright with combining *Besonnenheit* with creative rapture (*Enthusiasmus*) in a manner peculiar to genius: 'Genius, even in the highest degrees of rapture, works with rational awareness and freedom. He is penetrated by his subject-matter, elevated, inspired, but not controlled by it.'[25]

For Hoffmann, music is fundamentally a form of religious worship. He applies to music the religious understanding of visual art put forward by Wackenroder. In the essay 'Old and New Church Music', Hoffmann affirms that music proceeds from humanity's spiritual nature: 'Sound audibly expresses an awareness of the highest and holiest, of the spiritual power which enkindles the spark of life in the whole of nature' (C 355). Music reached a peak of achievement in the Counter-Reformation, especially in the work of Palestrina. His 'devout simplicity' was later shared by Alessandro Scarlatti (1660–1725) and Johann Sebastian Bach. The eighteenth century, however, was dominated by shallow Enlightenment thinking ('Aufklärerei', H II/1, 522) and superficial French culture (here Hoffmann, unusually, agrees with the xenophobia becoming current in his time). With the sole exception of Mozart's great Requiem, church music had, according to Hoffmann, been overtaken by 'mundane, ostentatious levity' and 'sickly sweetness' (C 370). Hoffmann saw hope, however, in the works of Haydn, Mozart and Beethoven, who 'evolved a new art', namely instrumental music. The unspoken implication is that instrumental music, even if ostensibly secular, is an act of religious worship of which church music is no longer capable.

Given his lofty conception of music, Hoffmann could only deplore the degeneration of music into drawing-room entertainment. In a fictional letter ascribed to a learned ape, ironic praise is lavished on the fashion for stretching the upper voice limit to produce an unnatural falsetto.[26] Even without such extravagances, Hoffmann, drawing on his extensive and often painful experience as a music teacher, complained bitterly in the persona of his alter ego Kreisler about how music in polite society was being consumed along with tea, punch, wine and ices (C 81). He lamented to his friends the necessity of teaching talentless young women, especially those with interfering mothers who substituted pieces of music of their own choice, chiding Hoffmann for their daughters' slow progress and comparing him unfavourably with other teachers (A 152). A little sketch, 'Der Musikfeind' ('The Music-Hater', 1814), presents somebody who does not share conventional taste in music but feels a 'hurricane' of emotions when hearing such great works as Gluck's *Iphigénie* operas, and is therefore ostracized for supposedly being unmusical, finding sympathy only from the true musician Kreisler (C 150).

The musical aesthetic that Hoffmann formulates also has a bearing on his writing. It is easy to apply to Hoffmann, as to

Beethoven, the stereotype of the Romantic genius creating his works in a state of literal or metaphorical intoxication and deficient self-control. This view of Hoffmann owes something to his habit of presenting himself as always with a glass in his hand.[27] It probably owes even more to Jacques Offenbach's opera *The Tales of Hoffmann*, which begins and ends by showing Hoffmann carousing in a tavern. However, the combination of creative rapture and rational awareness that Hoffmann ascribes to Shakespeare and Beethoven also powered his own writing. His fiction, though produced often at great speed and under pressure, was not carelessly dashed off; when read closely, the works reveal the utmost precision and coherence, even in recounting events that defy a complete rational explanation.[28]

Two Musical Narratives

Hoffmann's exalted conception of music finds expression also in his earliest fiction. When Rochlitz accepted the short narrative 'The Chevalier Gluck' for publication in 1809, he did so even though the *AMZ* did not normally publish fiction, and posterity has found it one of Hoffmann's most intriguing works. The story's narrator twice encounters a mysterious stranger in Berlin. The first time, at an open-air café in the Tiergarten, they listen to an orchestra playing the overture from Gluck's opera *Iphigénie en Aulide*; the second time, they meet outside a theatre where Gluck's *Armide* is being performed, and the stranger takes the narrator to his lodgings and shows him how the overture to *Armide* should be played. The stranger talks enigmatically of the 'realm of dreams' where a few 'crazy figures', having left the 'broad highway' of everyday life, may make contact with 'the eternal, ineffable' (H II/1, 24). He himself, he later reveals, sojourned in the realm of dreams, but on leaving it he profaned what should have been sacred, and was therefore condemned to wander among the living 'like a departed spirit' (H II/1, 30). At the end he appears in ceremonial dress and announces: 'I am the Chevalier Gluck!'

Commentators have wondered who the stranger is. He cannot really be Gluck, who died in 1787, 22 years before Hoffmann wrote the story. He twice compares himself to a departed spirit (H II/1, 26, 30), but the comparison implies that he is not literally one. Is he a madman who thinks he is Gluck, or a fantasy of the narrator? These questions are unanswerable. Hoffmann liked to imagine historical characters reappearing in later epochs. In *Meister Floh* (Master Flea, 1822) the seventeenth-century naturalists Antonie van Leeuwenhoek (1632–1723) and Jan Swammerdam (1637–1680) appear, without explanation, in nineteenth-century Frankfurt. In his notebooks Hoffmann imagined Frederick the Great educating a Spanish orphan who then went to Spain and became the famous dramatist Calderón, who died in 1680, some thirty years before Frederick's birth (H I, 790–91). As with these anachronisms, Gluck's appearance has simply to be accepted.

But why does Gluck blame himself for profaning the sacred? Although Gluck's popularity had declined since his death, Hoffmann thought very highly of him, considering him a 'giant' whose operas, unlike most contemporary works, attained 'tragic depth'.[29] The works Gluck composed during his endeavours to reform opera in Paris, including *Armide* and the two *Iphigénie* operas, were intended to attain a 'beautiful simplicity' without superfluous trimmings.[30] That corresponded to Hoffmann's own musical ideals. The sin that Gluck must expiate may therefore be that he wasted his lofty art on audiences who lacked the taste to appreciate it.

Much as Hoffmann admired Gluck, his favourite opera was Mozart's *Don Giovanni* (1787). While living in Bamberg between 1808 and 1813 he was able to see several performances that starred his friend the actor Franz von Holbein in the lead role.[31] 'Don Juan', Hoffmann's fictional reflection on *Don Giovanni*, first appeared in the *AMZ* in 1813 and was reprinted in *Fantasy-Pieces*. From its subtitle we learn that the narrator is the 'travelling enthusiast' who appears in several other Hoffmann texts. Writing to his friend Theodor, the enthusiast recounts a performance of *Don Giovanni* taking place in a theatre next to his hotel. A hidden door leads from his bedroom to a box in the theatre, where he is able to watch the performance alone, his solitary enjoyment broken only by a mysterious female figure who steals into his box during the first act.

The performance depicted is an ideal version of the opera as it ought to be. To the narrator's surprise, the opera, though produced in a German town, is sung in Italian. Don Giovanni appears as a tall, handsome, imposing figure with piercing eyes and a muscle twitching in his forehead that suggests the cynicism of Mephistopheles, the infernal emissary in Goethe's *Faust*. He clearly embodies satanic pride, internally tormented but scornful of the 'little people' around him (H II/1, 86). The enthusiast interprets him as a character endowed by nature with almost godlike qualities but caught in a conflict between divine and demonic forces. His insatiable yearning makes him seek satisfaction in the whole gamut of earthly experiences (like Faust), but without success. The Devil inspires him with 'the idea that through love, through the enjoyment of women, it is possible here on earth to satisfy what dwells in our bosoms as a heavenly promise, and is precisely that infinite yearning that places us in immediate contact with the supramundane' (H II/1, 93). Disappointed there too, he makes his erotic experiences 'no longer the satisfaction of his senses, but impious scorn of nature and the Creator' (H II/1, 93). Despising ordinary happiness, he deliberately destroys women by seducing and then discarding them, regarding this as a series of victories over the divine power. His ultimate triumph is the seduction of Donna Anna, an exceptional woman who might have saved him, but he infects her with his devilish sensuality. She feels that only Don Giovanni's death can bring peace to her soul, but such peace would itself be fatal to her. Once the Don has been carried down to hell, she will not be able to return to earthly life, and certainly not to her dull, timid fiancé Don Ottavio.

The woman who enters the narrator's box claims to be Donna Anna, though Anna is simultaneously performing on the stage. After the opera's end, the enthusiast leaves the box briefly to dine in the hotel, then returns to write his account. As the clock strikes two, he feels a warm breath, scents an Italian perfume and even hears Anna's voice. The next day, during lunch in the hotel, he learns that the singer who played Donna Anna died at exactly 2 a.m. As in 'Ritter Gluck', no explanation of these events is offered.

Among the interpretations of *Don Giovanni*, Hoffmann's has been called the most profound, ahead of that offered by Søren Kierkegaard in *Either/Or* (1843).[32] It has also been queried, since librettist Lorenzo Da Ponte's text does not actually say that Don Giovanni succeeds in seducing Donna Anna. However, Hoffmann's interpretation is based explicitly on the music rather than the text.[33] His narrator points out that the text, taken by itself, shows us merely the trivial exploits of a 'bon vivant' (H II/1, 92). The profundity is in the music, which only a kindred soul can understand: 'Only the poet understands the poet; only a romantic disposition can enter into the romantic' (H II/1, 92).

Bamberg and the Theatre

Hoffmann's reasonably comfortable and fulfilling life in Warsaw was brought to a sudden end when Napoleon's armies inflicted two humiliating defeats on Prussia at the battles of Jena and Auerstedt, both on 14 October 1806. On 28 November the French forces arrived in Warsaw. The law court where Hoffmann worked was suspended and all German government officials were summarily dismissed. Hoffmann sent Mischa and their daughter to stay with Mischa's family in Posen and hung on in Warsaw, hoping the situation might improve. In June 1807, however, Hoffmann and other German ex-officials were required either to sign a declaration of loyalty to Napoleon or leave Warsaw within a week. 'You can readily imagine', Hoffmann explained to Hippel, 'that every honest man chose the latter' (20 October 1807). He moved to Berlin, where he endured a difficult year, helped financially by a loan from Hippel but often living close to starvation and desperately seeking employment. Eventually he advertised in the newspapers, offering himself to any theatre as musical director, and received two offers, one from Lucerne and the other from Bamberg. He pursued the latter. The director of the Bamberg theatre, Count Julius von Soden, asked him as a trial of his abilities to compose music for Soden's libretto *Der Trank der Unsterblichkeit* (The Draught of Immortality); Hoffmann passed muster, and was engaged from 1 September 1808.[34]

Hoffmann's house in Bamberg at Schillerplatz 26, now a museum.

Bamberg was a new environment for Hoffmann. In contrast to the Protestant north, where he had been brought up, Bamberg, in central Germany, was a deeply Catholic town. Hoffmann felt neither the widespread Protestant aversion to Catholic worship nor the enthusiasm that led several leading Romantics – among them Zacharias Werner, who converted in 1810, took orders and ended his life as a fashionable preacher in Vienna – to adopt Catholicism. He enjoyed visiting the Capuchin monastery outside Bamberg and depicted a Benedictine monastery affectionately towards the end of *Murr*. In that novel he also portrayed satirically the sham court that existed in Bamberg. Bamberg had been an independent principality within the Holy Roman Empire until, like many other such territories, it was 'mediatized' by Napoleon – that is, incorporated within a larger unit, in this case the Kingdom of Bavaria. Its ruler, Duke Wilhelm, presided over a court that had only a ceremonial existence with no responsibility for government. Hoffmann was introduced at court and asked to provide a prologue for the celebration of the duchess's daughter's name day. As he reported cynically to Hitzig on 1 January 1809, 'I threw a horribly sentimental thing together and composed emotional music for it,' whereupon 'mother and daughter, weeping, embraced each other in the ducal box' and Hoffmann was rewarded with a handsome and very welcome fee. The duke's son Pius, who was mentally disturbed and prone to violent rages in which he attacked unoffending strangers, appears as Prince Ignaz in *Murr*.

The Bamberg theatre proved a severe disappointment. Just before Hoffmann arrived, Count Soden had handed over the directorship to an actor named Heinrich Cuno, whom Hoffmann described to Hitzig as 'an ignorant conceited windbag' (1 January 1809). Hoffmann found the quality of the singers and the orchestra dismayingly poor. His first task was to conduct Henri-Montan Berton's opera *Aline, Queen of Golconda* (1803). It had been an international success but, despite Hoffmann's efforts, failed dismally in Bamberg. Hoffmann was forced out of his post as director of music but was kept on as theatre composer. He supplemented his precarious income by teaching music, including giving singing lessons to five countesses, as he recounts in a letter of 1 January 1809. He also composed some major musical works: the *Miserere* for the Grand Duke Ferdinand, whose residence was in Würzburg, some 96 kilometres (60 mi.) west of Bamberg, and the score for Soden's operatic libretto *Dirna*, which was staged on 11 October 1809 and was also performed in Salzburg and Donauwörth.

Before long, Cuno drove the theatre into bankruptcy. Rather than let it close, its creditors insisted on a rescue package whereby the actors should stay on for the summer at two-thirds of their wages (letter to Hitzig, 25 May 1809). In September 1809 Soden resumed the management of the theatre, and a year later he handed it over to the actor Franz von Holbein, who happened to be an old friend of Hoffmann: they had seen much of each other in Berlin around 1799. In 1811–12 Hoffmann composed the music for Holbein's opera *Aurora*, but this led to yet another of his musical frustrations: the political upheavals of the time prevented the opera from being staged. It was accepted for performance in Vienna, and Hoffmann wrote a second score for it, but the score was never used (and was discovered only in 1962).[35]

Hoffmann and Holbein decided that Bamberg was the place where they had the chance to put on some striking plays. They thought above all of Calderón and of *The Devotion of the Cross*. Romantic readers found in this play a Catholic counterpart to the story of Oedipus. Its hero, Eusebio, born in mysterious circumstances, unwittingly commits incest with his sister Julia. Like Oedipus, he finds that fate reveals his crime but also permits atonement. Whereas Oedipus suffers self-knowledge and self-punishment, Eusebio is redeemed at the foot of the cross under which he was born. Julia finds his corpse and embraces the cross, which flies aloft with her to meet the radiant figure of Eusebio among the clouds. The play was an enormous success among its largely Catholic audience, not only because of its message but because Hoffmann's skilful use of stage machinery secured a complete dramatic illusion – something he considered essential to the effect of any play.

It was in Bamberg too that Hoffmann's literary career began to take off, although he still considered himself first and foremost a composer. He formed an important, though not very close, friendship with Carl Friedrich Kunz (1785–1849), a wine merchant who owned a substantial book collection. With Hoffmann's help, Kunz enlarged his collection and made it into a public library. He also set up as a publisher. He encouraged Hoffmann to put together various scattered writings as a book. This eventually included two series of musical writings, including the great essay 'Beethoven's Instrumental Music', under the heading *Kreisleriana* (from *Fantasy-Pieces*) which refers to Hoffmann's fictional musician Kreisler; there were also some short narratives, including 'Ritter Gluck', 'Don Juan', *Der goldne Topf* (The Golden Pot) and 'Nachricht von den neuesten Schicksalen des Hundes Berganza' ('News of the Most Recent Experiences of the Dog Berganza'). The last is presented as a semi-comic continuation of Cervantes's story 'The Dogs' Colloquy' (1613), a dialogue between two dogs, Berganza and Cipión, who are temporarily endowed with speech. Hoffmann's Berganza, inexplicably transplanted to modern Germany, not only tells his human interlocutor a story but expresses firm opinions about art and theatre. One of his dicta importantly supplements Hoffmann's musical aesthetics:

Bamberg physician Dr Christian Pfeufer examines a blister on the tip of the tongue of Carl Friedrich Kunz, while Hoffmann himself draws the scene, 1809–13.

> Art has no higher purpose than to kindle in man that pleasure which frees his whole being from all earthly torment, all the burdensome pressure of daily life, as though from filthy dross, and elevates him in such a way that he can raise his head proudly and gladly to behold the divine and even come in contact with it. (H II/1, 168)

Julia and the Consequences

Towards the end of 1810 Hoffmann became infatuated with his fourteen-year-old pupil Juliane ('Julia') Marc. According to Kunz, she was an intelligent, unaffected girl, more a Rubens than a Raphael type (that is, tending to plumpness). Juliane never returned Hoffmann's feelings in the slightest (A 189), but he became obsessed with her and talked about her endlessly. In his diary he used the abbreviation 'Ktch' when talking about her, a nickname alluding to the play by Heinrich von Kleist, *Das Käthchen von Heilbronn* (Käthchen of Heilbronn, 1810), in which a young woman is linked by a magnetic bond to the male protagonist and follows him around incessantly (very unlike Julia). On 3 February 1812 he even fantasized about a joint suicide, presumably recalling how Kleist, three months earlier, had shot his terminally ill lover Henriette Vogel and then himself beside the Wannsee near Berlin. Julia, however, was destined by her widowed mother to marry the Hamburg merchant Johann Gerhard Graepel (fifteen years her senior), whom Kunz describes as a prematurely aged debauchee whose every word betrayed his mental 'imbecility' (A 206).

On 6 September 1812 Julia's mother, Julia, Graepel, Kunz, Hoffmann and Mischa all went on an excursion to Pommersfelden near Bamberg. Hoffmann, by his own admission, got very drunk and denounced Graepel, who himself was so drunk that he fell to the ground.[36] The next day Hoffmann wrote Frau Marc a letter of apology; she put an end to his music lessons. Julia married Graepel on 3 December; Hoffmann's diary records 'Julie's wedding-day *con questo maledetto mercante*' ('with that accursed merchant'; H I, 438). The marriage was unhappy and would have ended in divorce if

Hoffmann's drawing of a burning castle for a production in Bamberg of Kleist's *Das Käthchen von Heilbronn*, September 1811.

Graepel had not died, aged 41, in 1821, whereupon Julia married her cousin Ludwig Marc. She and Hoffmann had no further contact. A year prior to Graepel's death, however, in 1820, Hoffmann had been horrified to learn that Julia had left her husband of eight years after undergoing 'nameless sufferings' from the 'shameless bestiality of the detested weakling'. He asked his Bamberg friend Friedrich Speyer (1782–1839) to convey to Julia a message: 'the angelic image of all heartfelt kindness, all the heavenly charm of a true womanly disposition, of childlike virtue, that beamed upon me in that wretched period of Acherontic darkness, can never leave me even in my dying breath' (1 May 1820).

His experience with Julia undoubtedly meant a great deal to Hoffmann. But, as his note of 1 May suggests, there was something strained and artificial about it. He saw her through the lenses provided by two of his favourite dramatic heroines: Kleist's Käthchen and Shakespeare's Juliet.[37] He turned her into literature, most memorably as Julia in *Murr*; she may also have helped to inspire the idealized Clara in his short story 'Der Sandmann' ('The Sandman', 1816). Her earliest literary transformation is in the 'Berganza' story. The dog tells how his mistress Cäcilia (the name, as we have seen, not only of the patron saint of music but of Hoffmann's baby daughter) has been compelled by her greedy mother to marry a wealthy but debauched merchant, Georg, whom Berganza hates. On their wedding night Berganza hides under the marital bed. Georg appears, disgustingly drunk, and mauls his wife brutally, whereupon Berganza seizes him by the leg, pulls him out of the room and savages him. Berganza is Hoffmann's surrogate, embodying his feeling of being despised (especially as Hoffmann was a very small man), registering Cäcilia/Julia's sexual desirability and taking revenge on his behalf.

Dresden and Napoleon

Holbein and Hoffmann could not save the Bamberg theatre from bankruptcy. In February 1812 Holbein moved to a position in Würzburg. Hoffmann survived by offering music lessons until he was given the post of musical director for the opera company run by Joseph Seconda (1761–1820), which was based in Dresden and Leipzig, the two main cities of Saxony. Hoffmann took up this new post on 21 April 1813. He arrived in Dresden on 25 April but had to follow the company to Leipzig, returning to Dresden on 25 June.

What Hoffmann had not foreseen was that Saxony was now a war zone. After Napoleon's defeat in Russia, Prussia broke the treaty with France that it had concluded under duress in 1807 and declared war on France on 13 March 1813. Russia, Prussia and soon afterwards Austria formed an anti-France alliance, supported at sea by Britain. In May 1813 Napoleon, who had rebuilt an army of some 400,000 men, twice defeated his opponents in battles on Saxon territory and, after a brief armistice, defeated them again at the Battle of Dresden on 26–7 August. Since this battle was indecisive, Napoleon sought a further confrontation at Leipzig; in this 'Battle of the Nations' (16–19 October 1813) he was defeated, and having refused the peace terms offered by the allied nations, he was transported in April 1814 to exile on the island of Elba.

From May to November 1813, Hoffmann and Mischa were living in an occupied and besieged city. His diary conveys how, remarkably, normal life went on, despite food shortages and anxiety about the future. The company rehearsed and performed operas. Cafés and taverns stayed open and were well patronized. On 26 August, Hoffmann and his friend the actor J. G. Keller watched the battle from Hoffmann's window while enjoying some wine. Hoffmann later wrote up the experience for the benefit of his Bamberg friends in a document entitled 'Drei verhängnisvolle Monate!' ('Three Fateful Months!'), which, despite its name, is incomplete, covering only two weeks – but then, what weeks! Part of it runs:

> We [Hoffmann and Keller] were sitting quite cheerfully, looking out of the window with a glass of wine in our hands, when a grenade fell and exploded in the middle of the market square – at the same moment a Westphalian soldier who was about to pump water dropped dead with his head smashed – and some distance away a respectably dressed citizen – The latter seemed about to pick himself up – but his body had been torn open, his guts were hanging out, he dropped dead (N.B. five minutes later the Emperor [Napoleon] rode across the New Market, just where the citizen had been hit, towards the Pirna Gate) – at the Church of Our Lady three more people were severely wounded by the same grenade – the actor Keller dropped his glass – I emptied mine and exclaimed: 'What is life! unable to stand a bit of red-hot iron, how weak is human nature!' (H I, 806)

Anyone who knows Hoffmann's novella *The Golden Pot*, subtitled 'A Modern Fairy-Tale' and set in a peaceful Dresden, which Hoffmann began writing on 26 November 1813, will feel somewhat shocked to see places familiar from the story appearing as sites of violent death and devastation. In the passage just quoted, Hoffmann is of course stylizing himself, but his coolness accompanies a certain taste for the macabre.[38]

E.T.A. Hoffmann, *Die Exorcisten* (The Exorcists), 1814, a political cartoon showing Lady Gallia (France) freed from demonic posession by the allied forces, who blow the Devil (Napoleon) away.

Although Hoffmann's friends attest to his total lack of interest in politics, he admitted in January 1814 that 'a dark and unhappy age has seized men with its iron fist, and the pain squeezes from them sounds that were formerly alien to them.'[39] It is clear from his diaries that he cared little whether Napoleon or the allies won, so long as peace was restored.[40] However, he increasingly regarded Napoleon as a destructive, even demonic figure. He set eyes on

Napoleon several times during the siege of Dresden and noted in his diary on 30 August 1813 the French ruler's 'frightful tyrannical gaze' (Hoffmann's emphasis). In a powerful short text published as an anonymous pamphlet in 1814, "Die Vision auf dem Schlachtfelde bei Dresden' ('The Vision on the Battlefield of Dresden'), Hoffmann writes of a dark pillar of smoke arising from the battlefield and assuming Napoleon's shape; the tyrant is seized by a dragon and condemned by a thunderous voice: 'Your punishment and your torment will be everlasting!' (H II/1, 482). And in 'Der Dey von Elba in Paris' ('The Dey of Elba in Paris', 1814), inspired by Napoleon's escape from Elba, Hoffmann satirizes what would nowadays be called news junkies and conspiracy theorists, then evokes patriotic unity among German citizens, one of whom says: 'Buonaparte's great demonic principle is that all men are either weaklings or villains and must be trampled underfoot' (H II/2, 415). These texts are mild specimens of the upsurge of patriotism and nationalism that accompanied the so-called War of Liberation against the French. The second, by the emphasis it places on 'citizens' (*Bürger*), may imply a plea for civic equality as opposed to aristocratic caste society.

The day after his arrival in Dresden, Hoffmann unexpectedly ran into his old friend Hippel, whom he had not seen for nine years. They met in Linke's Restaurant, another locale familiar from *The Golden Pot*. Hippel had re-entered public service and was now on the staff of Count (later Prince) Hardenberg, the Prussian chancellor. Their meeting was fortunate, for in February 1814 Hoffmann fell out with Seconda over a trivial issue and was dismissed. He hoped to earn money from writing: he completed *The Golden Pot* in the same month and included it in the collection *Fantasy-Pieces*, which Kunz published in 1814 and 1815, and he set to work on the Gothic thriller *Die Elixiere des Teufels* (The Devil's Elixirs, 1815–16). But writing promised at best a meagre and insecure income. Reluctantly, Hoffmann decided to follow Hippel back into the law. Hippel helped him to secure a position, initially unpaid, in Prussian government service.

E.T.A. Hoffmann, in the manner of Dante's Virgil, shows the landscape around Bamberg to the physician Dr Adalbert Friedrich Marcus, drawing with opaque colours on cardboard by Hoffmann, 1809–13.

2

Bamberg: Medicine, Psychology and Fiction

Hoffmann's period in Bamberg, from September 1808 to April 1813, decisively shaped his fiction by opening up to him the world of Romantic medicine and psychology. The Bamberg General Hospital, opened in 1789, had as its director Adalbert Friedrich Marcus (1753–1816), a leading medical reformer. Like many contemporaries, Marcus rejected the old humoral pathology whose main method of treatment was bloodletting in order to rectify the balance of fluids in the body. Continuing the late Enlightenment's interest in the 'whole person', he explored many new approaches to illness and its treatment that drew on natural forces. These included galvanism, the generation of electricity in biological organisms, seen in the South American electric eel; the unexplained psychic rapport between often distant people, found in accounts of telepathy; and such phenomena as somnambulism (sleepwalking), which seemed to reveal an unconscious psychic activity. Hoffmann became a close friend of Marcus, who introduced him to Bamberg's polished society, and of another doctor with similar interests, Friedrich Speyer.

Through Marcus and Speyer, Hoffmann got to know the extensive literature on insanity and on intriguing phenomena such as animal magnetism, somnambulism and clairvoyance. He also borrowed books on these subjects from Kunz's large library. The concept of animal magnetism originated with Franz Anton Mesmer (1734–1815), who created a sensation, first in Vienna and later in Paris, through his displays of hypnotism (often called mesmerism after him).[1] He gave the name 'animal magnetism' to cures attributed to a mysterious fluid pervading the universe,

E.T.A. Hoffmann, self-portrait with physiognomic explanations, n.d.

which was present also in his own body and produced magnetic streams in the patient that swept away the patient's disease. Disease was said to result from the unequal distribution of this fluid in the human body; equilibrium could be restored with the help of certain techniques. Mesmer conceived the universal fluid as analogous to Newton's universal gravitation and called it *gravitatio universalis*; it existed in several forms, one being electricity.[2] Hoffmann's understanding of magnetism was derived less from Mesmer than from one of his followers, the Marquis de Puységur (1751–1825), who gave the movement a new direction by discovering 'magnetic sleep'. He found that he could put patients into a kind of sleep in which they could speak and answer questions with more intelligence than they showed when awake. Thus magnetism no longer rested on materialist assumptions, but rather on a psychological theory. The sympathetic rapport between magnetizer and subject was all-important. Ominously, however, this relationship was one of unequal power. The magnetic subject appeared to be entirely under the magnetizer's sway.

In Hoffmann's collection of stories titled *Die Serapions-Brüder* (The Serapion Brethren, 1819–21), in which several characters recount stories to one another, magnetism is the subject of a long discussion among the four original members of the eponymous brotherhood. Their views range from Lothar's qualified scepticism to Cyprian's interpretation of magnetism as the power of 'our psychic

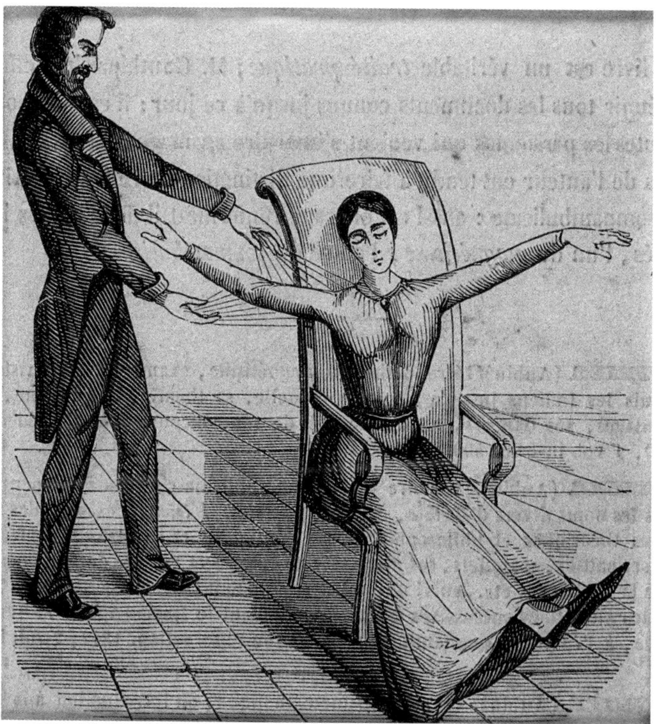

A mesmerist using animal magnetism on a woman, who responds by falling into convulsions, 1847.

principle' in which we hear 'the mysterious music of the spheres, which is the great immutable vital principle of nature itself' (H IV, 317–18). Theodor, mediating between these extremes, reports on his own experiences as a witness to magnetic operations. In one case, he becomes convinced that the magnetism is fraudulent, but that the fraud is being practised not by the physician but by his patient, who pretends to become clairvoyant in magnetic sleep: when it is proposed to test her unconscious condition by applying red-hot irons to her feet, she promptly wakes up. The other case is conducted by an unnamed physician who is easily identifiable as Dr Marcus. Here the patient, a peasant girl, convinces Theodor of the reality of magnetism, not only by revealing otherwise inexplicable knowledge but by speaking in the educated accent of the physician instead of her own thick rural dialect. Theodor is horrified, however, by the somnambulist girl's complete subjection to the will of the magnetizer. Dr Marcus evidently shared his unease, for he conducted such operations only rarely and secretly. The main conclusion is that the power exercised by the magnetizer makes magnetism an extremely dangerous practice. When performed, as often, before a large audience, it flatters the patient's vanity by making them the centre of a theatrical performance and unleashes self-induced fantasies such as are known from documented cases of supposed demonic possession: Theodor mentions the famous outbreak of mass hysteria that occurred in the convent of Loudun in 1634.[3]

The potential of magnetism for evil is exposed in 'Der Magnetiseur' ('The Magnetizer'), written in 1813. The story has a strangely fragmented form. First, four members of a family group – the elderly Baron, his son Ottmar and daughter Marie, and their friend the painter Franz Bickert – discuss apparent magnetic phenomena, including the magnetic powers shown by Ottmar's friend Alban. When Marie falls into persistent anxiety, Alban casts her into a magnetic sleep from which she wakes up refreshed. There follow various letters. In one, Marie confides to a friend that Alban is absorbing her into his own being. A letter from Alban to a university friend confirms that this is his intention and reveals his contempt for conventional morality, his belief that life is a remorseless struggle and his ambition to attain 'absolute command over the spiritual principle of life' (H II/1, 213). He despises his hosts and is working to strengthen the spiritual bond he senses between himself and Marie; he deliberately induced her anxiety in order to receive the credit for curing her. When Marie is about to marry her fiancé, she drops dead at the altar; Alban vanishes, her father dies of grief and her brother is killed in a duel. We learn all this only later from scraps of a diary kept by old Bickert. Thus the disjointed form of the story enacts the destruction wantonly brought about by the power-hungry Alban.

Alban had many counterparts, both in real life and in fiction. The late eighteenth century saw the emergence of many charismatic charlatans who convinced large numbers of people that they had supernatural powers. The most famous was Giuseppe Balsamo (1743–1795), who assumed the name Count Alessandro di Cagliostro and travelled around Europe, claiming that he possessed the secrets of ancient 'Egyptian Freemasonry'.[4] He was marginally involved in the Diamond Necklace Affair that brought Marie Antoinette into disrepute, and was briefly imprisoned in the Bastille. His alleged powers included the ability to pass through locked doors, an ability attributed in 'The Magnetizer' to Alban. In 'The Sandman', Nathanael compares the new professor of physics, Spalanzani, to a well-known picture of Cagliostro (*GP* 96). He has a fictional counterpart in the mysterious Armenian who manages to dominate the protagonist in Schiller's horror novel *The Ghost-Seer*; Theodor in 'The Entail' attests to the popularity of Schiller's story, 'which, like so many others at that time, I carried in my pocket' (*Tales* 192). And Hoffmann even implies an association between the powerful gaze of the charlatan and the appearance of Napoleon, whose 'frightful tyrannical gaze' he observed through his telescope in Dresden.[5]

Despite his roots in the Enlightenment, Dr Marcus shared with contemporaries the Romantic desire to overcome artificial boundaries such as that between the mind and the body, and to understand the universe as an interconnected whole. He found powerful support in the 'nature philosophy' (*Naturphilosophie*) of the post-Kantian thinker F.W.J. Schelling (1775–1854), who in 1798 had been appointed to a chair at the University of Jena, thanks to advocacy by Goethe, and who often visited Marcus in Bamberg. Schelling's *Von der Weltseele* (On the World Soul, 1798) offers an account of the principles that structure the universe, which are manifested in physical and chemical processes. It made a strong impression on the group of early Romantic writers in Jena, particularly Novalis. Hoffmann read it in 1813 and must have done so carefully, for he speaks of making a 'study' of it (26 July 1813). He was clearly attracted by Schelling's argument that the basic principle in nature is 'universal dualism', which he also calls 'universal doubleness' (*Duplizität*).[6] All motion in nature results from the interaction of opposed forces. Even light, the most fundamental force in nature, is double, because the light streaming from the Sun encounters material bodies as soon as it approaches Earth. Electricity is pre-eminently dual, because it consists of positive and negative charges. Schelling's basic idea of duality occurs at key points in Hoffmann's writing, as when one of the Serapion Brethren speaks of 'the doubleness [*Duplizität*] by which alone our earthly being is determined' (H IV, 68).

Schelling's cosmogony was elaborated in another book, *Ansichten von der Nachtseite der Naturwissenschaft* (Views of the Night-Side of Natural Science, 1808), which Hoffmann read with great enthusiasm. This work was originally delivered as public lectures in Dresden by Gotthilf Heinrich Schubert (1780–1860), a prominent thinker and a friend of Schelling, Marcus and Goethe.[7] In the *Ansichten* Schubert offers nothing less than a history of humanity, from its primeval unity with nature to its estrangement and thence to a future reunion in a higher form of existence. Ancient mythologies retain memories of a golden age when humanity lived in harmony with nature; in a fruitful region called Atlantis, situated near the North Pole, humans enjoyed a warm climate because Earth had not yet cooled down. Estrangement brought about warfare, the destruction of nature and the present situation, in which knowledge about nature in the impoverished form of natural science simply confirms our remoteness from it. Those scientists who undertake responsible investigations of magnetism, however, are disclosing the night-side of nature (what would later be called the unconscious) in magnetic sleep, clairvoyance and somnambulism. They reveal that our destiny is to regain, thanks to conscious effort, the innocent unity with nature that we possessed at the beginning of our history. Even death may be the gateway to a new form of existence. The signs of spiritual exaltation sometimes shown by dying people are not premonitions of death, but 'moments when human nature lifts anchor to set out for a more beautiful home, and the vibrations of a new existence begin to stir'.[8] Schubert's historical narrative, eloquently delivered, conforms to a familiar Romantic conception of history as triadic: an initial golden age is followed by a fall into the world we know, but with the prospect of regaining paradise on a higher level that restores primeval innocence but combines it with the intellectual maturity and self-awareness that humanity will ultimately attain.[9]

The Golden Pot

Hoffmann's fascination with occult phenomena is prominent in his first book publication, *Fantasy-Pieces*. Of its four volumes, published by Kunz in Bamberg, the first two appeared in May 1814, the third, consisting of *The Golden Pot*, in November, and the fourth in April or May 1815. The book is a miscellany; its contents, some of it reprinted from magazines and some new, include many essays, notes and letters attributed to the musician Kreisler, essays on music including 'Beethoven's Instrumental Music', and numerous works of fiction, among them 'Ritter Gluck', 'Don Juan', 'Berganza', *The Golden Pot* and 'The Magnetizer'; they also include a story made famous by Offenbach's opera *The Tales of Hoffmann*, 'Die Geschichte vom verlorenen Spiegelbilde' ('The Tale of the Lost Reflection', 1815), in which the guileless Erasmus Spikher, travelling in Italy, becomes besotted with the courtesan Giulietta and is persuaded by the devilish Doctor Dapertutto (Italian for 'everywhere') to give her his mirror-image.

The book testifies to Hoffmann's enthusiasm not only for music and literature but for visual art. It begins with a short tribute to the

Jacques Callot, 'Captain of the Barons', frontispiece from the series of etchings *Les Gueux* (The Beggars), 1617–27.

artist Jacques Callot (1592–1635), who was famous for his etchings *Les Grandes Misères de la guerre* (1633), depicting the horrors of the French invasion of his native Lorraine. Although Hoffmann's recent experience of war must have heightened his appreciation of Callot, he highlights what he called the latter's 'irony'. Callot portrays beggars, peasants and musicians with 'romantic originality', which ironically reveals humanity's animal nature while gesturing towards a profound, ineffable significance. Hoffmann ends by hinting at his own artistic practice:

> Could not a poet or writer to whom the figures of ordinary life appear in his inner romantic realm of the spirit, and who portrays them in the light in which they are bathed as though in a strange and wondrous garb – could he not at least excuse himself by naming this master and saying that he wanted to work in Callot's manner? (H IV, 18)

Hoffmann thus formulates a theme that will run through his fiction: the discrepancy between surface reality and the mysterious depths beneath. This corresponds to the philosophical dualism that Hoffmann read about in Schelling and Schubert. These philosophers provided material for *The Golden Pot*, which he wrote between November 1813 and February 1814. On planning the story, Hoffmann told Kunz not to expect anything like the *Thousand and One Nights*: the story would be 'fairy-like and wondrous, but stepping boldly into ordinary life' (19 August 1813).

Dualism is fundamental to *The Golden Pot*, which evokes two realities. One is the everyday world of Dresden, where the student Anselmus is unfortunate, accident-prone and unemployed. Dresden is inhabited by people whom some Romantic writers would dismiss as philistines, a judgement that would be unfair, for Anselmus's friends – the Paulmanns and Heerbrand – are cultivated, convivial and musical.[10] The second reality is evoked in a passage early in the Fourth Vigil, which, so Hoffmann told Kunz, expresses 'the idea which I intended to convey' (16 January 1814).[11] The reader is reminded of the 'fairy realm of glorious wonders', which we sometimes see in our dreams, and urged to 'believe that this magnificent realm is much nearer at hand than you had previously thought; and that is what I heartily wish you to believe, and what the strange story of Anselmus is supposed to convey' (GP 20–21). The 'sustained irony' (4 March 1814) that Hoffmann ascribed to his tale encourages the reader to inhabit both dimensions, the mundane world of Dresden and the wondrous world of Atlantis.[12]

The wondrous appears at the very beginning, when Anselmus in his haste knocks over a basket of apples that an old woman is offering for sale and is cursed in mysterious language: 'into glass you'll soon pass' (GP 1). He gives the apple-seller the money he had saved for a visit to Linke's Restaurant. Denied access to conventional social life by his clumsiness, he instead sits by the river and smokes his pipe. There he hears strange voices from the foliage of an elder tree and finds that they belong to three little green snakes, one of whom gazes at him with beautiful eyes. Hoffmann is here drawing on the superstition that if you fall asleep under an elder tree you will have a vision of your future lover, as in Kleist's *Käthchen von Heilbronn*, the play with which Hoffmann associated Julia Marc. The yearning gaze of the snake, who will later be revealed as the charming maiden Serpentina, is a positive counterpart to the sinister gaze of magnetizers like Alban.[13]

Henceforth Anselmus behaves in an increasingly eccentric manner, which makes his friends wonder whether he is mad. He is found clutching the trunk of the elder tree by townsfolk, who assume he is an intoxicated divinity student. Crossing the Elbe, he almost leaps out of the boat because he sees three snakes swimming in the water. Heerbrand recommends him to the royal archivist Lindhorst as a copyist, but when he finally goes to Lindhorst's house, he is presently found unconscious outside the door, being tended by the apple-seller; it appears that the door-knocker bore the woman's face and turned into a boa constrictor, which almost crushed Anselmus to death. Some commentators, noting that Anselmus's behaviour corresponds closely to the symptoms of insanity listed in the medical textbooks

Sir Richard Colt Hoare and John Warwick Smith, *The City of Dresden*, *c.* 1817, watercolour drawing.

Hoffmann knew, have assumed that he is literally mad, and that his extraordinary experiences can be interpreted as visual and auditory hallucinations.[14] However, these events are recounted not from Anselmus's point of view but the narrator's. Anselmus's experiences are presented to us as being just as real as their everyday setting in Dresden. He is gradually learning to live in duality, in two dimensions, the everyday and the wondrous.

The archivist Lindhorst already inhabits two dimensions. He is a salamander – not a lizard, but an elemental spirit who for his transgressions has been banished from the timeless realm of Atlantis and obliged to accept the restrictions of human life. Hoffmann took 'Atlantis' from Schubert; when it is evoked in the Twelfth Vigil it is described as containing forests of palm trees, just like the ancient realm near the North Pole evoked in the *Ansichten*. The salamander is one of the nature spirits that Renaissance scholars supposed to inhabit the four elements: we hear also of an earth spirit or gnome (*GP* 56), while Lindhorst's daughter Serpentina suggests both a nymph (water spirit) and a sylph (air spirit).[15] Lindhorst can only be recalled from his earthly exile if each of his three daughters marries a young man with a truly poetic disposition – a rare find in the present unpoetic age. He has tried out several young men already, and all have failed the test (copying a manuscript). Anselmus, set to copy what appears to be an Arabian manuscript, is helped by the youngest daughter, Serpentina, whose beautiful eyes he saw in the elder tree. The archivist is impressed by his flawless copying and promises that if he completes his task successfully, he and Serpentina will be married and receive the golden pot as a wedding present; but to enter the higher life in Atlantis, he must resist the malign powers conspiring against him.

These malign powers are also able to make use of the everyday world. Veronika Paulmann, who hopes to marry Anselmus and thus become eventually the wife of a *Hofrat* (court councillor), enlists the help of the apple-seller, who turns out to be her former nurse Liese, now living in a little house with a black cat as her familiar. The intrepid Veronika attends a magical ceremony in which Liese creates a magic mirror. This mirror establishes a kind of magnetic rapport between her and Anselmus. Whenever he looks into it, Anselmus feels drawn back to the everyday world and loses faith in the reality of the archivist's world. Thus Veronika paradoxically uses magic to entrap Anselmus in a one-dimensional world that denies the reality of magic.

As a result of Veronika's influence, Anselmus's faith in the archivist's world weakens. He misses his next appointment with Lindhorst and is instead drawn by the Paulmann family into a punch-drinking session, which becomes riotous. Intoxicated by the punch, Anselmus talks wildly about the archivist being a salamander, and Veronika, Heerbrand and even Veronika's father, the prosaic schoolmaster Paulmann, join in the revelry, until an emissary from the archivist comes to remind Anselmus to appear on the following day. To most of those present, the emissary looks like a little man in a grey suit with a hooked nose, but Anselmus recognizes him as the parrot that inhabits the archivist's house.

On his next visit to the archivist's house, Anselmus no longer perceives anything wondrous in it. The talking birds who greeted him previously now seem to be merely chattering sparrows, and the archivist a silly old man. From the standpoint of rationality, he has regained his senses. But in the dual perspective that the story requires, he is profoundly deluded. Nemesis soon comes: the script he is meant to copy no longer makes sense to him, and he allows a large blot to fall on the manuscript. As his punishment, he is confined in a crystal bottle on a shelf in the archivist's library.

In this supreme trial, the penitent Anselmus regains his faith in Serpentina and the wondrous. Her influence changes the crystal, through which only iridescent lights can be seen, into transparent glass, affording Anselmus room to breathe. Next to him on the shelf are five other bottles containing young men; these other victims do not realize they are in bottles but imagine themselves to be strolling about Dresden and having a good time (rather like the deluded majority of the human population kept trapped in an advanced simulation in the Wachowskis' film *The Matrix* (1999)). They typify the normal, one-dimensional reality of the story: most people go about their business without realizing that the other, wondrous dimension exists and disparage those who believe in the wondrous as being mad.

After a pitched battle between the archivist and Liese, supported respectively by the parrot and the black cat, the archivist's side is victorious and Anselmus, released, plunges from the shelf into Serpentina's arms.

Commentators disagree about how to interpret this conclusion. Some think that in the 'real' world Anselmus has been standing on the Elbe Bridge alongside the other young men, and that he commits suicide by plunging into the river.[16] But, in the story's reality, the young men are not standing on the bridge but imprisoned in bottles; their conception of 'reality' is one-dimensional and therefore illusory. As far as the other inhabitants of Dresden are concerned, Anselmus has vanished, and Veronika can marry Heerbrand, who has now attained the desired status of *Hofrat*. She asks Heerbrand to take her magic mirror, which broke in two when Liese died, and throw it off the Elbe Bridge. This may imply that Anselmus's corpse is lying under the bridge; but it is a very slight hint. One way or another, however, he has gone to Atlantis, and, as the vision in the Twelfth Vigil reveals, is enjoying happiness with Serpentina and the golden pot, which itself may be understood as symbolizing a combination of the magical and the natural.[17]

Anselmus's transition to Atlantis concludes not only his earthly life but the mythic narrative of which his biography forms a part. That narrative has three stages. The first is recounted by Lindhorst in a tavern to an audience who know him only as the archivist. It is a creation myth, freely elaborated from Schubert's *Ansichten*. The creative spirit brings the world forth from water. The natural world contains a dynamic principle, embodied by the black hill that, touched by the sun, produces a fiery lily. The lily yearns for something beyond nature and falls in love with the youth Phosphorus, the spiritual principle of light. The union of nature with spirit leads to the lily's death in a *Liebestod* (an arch-Romantic concept, exemplified at the end of Wagner's *Tristan und Isolde*), but she gives birth to a new being – consciousness, which, unable to find a home in the world, is captured by the black dragon, symbolizing the lower, sensual aspect of nature. The lily is reborn, but into a state of twofold alienation: cut off from her former unity with nature, yet unable to reach her spiritual goal, represented by Phosphorus. This alienation is overcome by the victory of Phosphorus over the dragon. The lily is freed from alienation and united with nature in love, on a higher level than before. All the natural elements pay homage to her, implying that nature has been united with consciousness and is able not only to experience but to enjoy 'the holy harmony of all living things' (GP 83).

In the second iteration of the myth, recounted by Serpentina in the Eighth Vigil, the role of Phosphorus is played by the salamander, her father. Finding that the consummation of his love destroys his beloved, the green snake, he ravages the garden and is banished from Atlantis to the human world, 'in that unhappy time when the degenerate race of men will no longer understand the language of nature' (GP 55). He is reunited with the green snake, and they produce three daughters, each of whom must find and marry a young man with 'a child-like poetic spirit' (GP 56). Anselmus is such a young man; he shows it by his ability to hear and see the three snakes and briefly to understand the language of nature. His story is the third iteration of the myth. The myth thus encloses the Dresden narrative, just as ordinary human life, we are to learn, is enclosed in the dimension of the wondrous.

In the final Vigil the narrator moves into the foreground. Lindhorst, annoyed at having his story published, invites the narrator to his house. Sitting at the very table where Anselmus copied manuscripts, the narrator is treated by Lindhorst to a bowl of arrack (spirits distilled from the coconut palm, which Lindhorst has growing in his house). Under its influence, the narrator has a vision of Anselmus in Atlantis, and on returning to normal consciousness feels depressed. Lindhorst, however, reassures him that he has just been in Atlantis, and that he retains 'a pretty farm there, as the poetic property of your mind' (*GP* 83). Atlantis therefore is not only a remote realm; it is available to anyone through the exercise of the imagination. This conclusion is ambiguous. Does it affirm the reality of Atlantis? Or does it intimate that Atlantis, however delightful, only exists in fantasy? The reader is left with the final (rhetorical?) question: 'is Anselmus's happiness anything other than life in poetry, where the holy harmony of all things is revealed as the deepest secret of nature?' (*GP* 83).

'The Sandman'

Commentators have often pointed out that 'The Sandman', completed in November 1815, resembles a negative mirror image of *The Golden Pot*. In both stories, the protagonist finds himself caught in a conflict between two women, one belonging to the everyday human world, the other to the fantastical: Anselmus between Veronika and Serpentina, Nathanael between Clara and the automaton Olimpia.[18] Lindhorst, as Serpentina's father, corresponds to Spalanzani, Olimpia's creator. Like Lindhorst, who is both a salamander and an archivist, Spalanzani's accomplice Coppelius has multiple identities: as a small-town lawyer, the Sandman of nursery stories and apparently also a man known as Coppola, a spectacle-seller. One could go further: S. S. Prawer has called 'The Sandman' a 'reversal or "Zurücknahme"' of *The Golden Pot*, implying that the later story retracts the message of the earlier by contrasting everyday life not with a wondrous other reality but with a sinister world of terror and madness.[19]

Both stories, moreover, ask what counts as reality. Instead of the dualism in *The Golden Pot*, which assigns equal reality to both Dresden and Atlantis, 'The Sandman' offers something more perplexing. The narrator tells us that he was uncertain how to begin the story. He might have used the standard fairy tale opening, 'Once upon a time . . .', or begun prosaically: 'In the small provincial town of S. there lived . . .'. Alternatively, he might have plunged *in medias res* with: '"Go to the Devil!" cried the student Nathanael.' Each opening implies a different conception of reality. The fairy-tale opening would imply a mythic world in which the existence of the demonic Sandman and the devilish Coppelius is unproblematic. The prosaic opening would introduce a realist narrative in which the Sandman, and the mysterious behaviour ascribed to Coppelius, can only be illusory. The third would present a highly dramatic narrative in which the characters' turbulent reactions to terrifying events rule out narratorial reflection on them.

Rejecting all three openings, the narrator decides not to begin the story at all, and instead presents the reader with three letters exchanged among the characters. These letters themselves offer different views about the nature of reality.[20] Nathanael writes to his friend Lothar with an account of his traumatic childhood recollections. These centre on an associate of his father's, the advocate Coppelius, whom the children hated. The young Nathanael identified him with the Sandman who in his nurse's stories was said to peck out the eyes of children who refuse to go to sleep. One night, in order to see the Sandman, he hid and watched his father and Coppelius doing something that involved a fireplace, a blue flame and a pair of tongs. Coppelius called: 'Bring the eyes!' whereupon Nathanael screamed in terror; Coppelius seized him, threatened to tear out his eyes and, when Nathanael's father pleaded for his son, contented himself with unscrewing the boy's limbs and placing them in different sockets, only to conclude: 'They don't fit properly! It was all right as it was! The Old Man knew what he was doing!' (*GP* 91). Nathanael fainted; on waking, he found himself being reassured by his mother. Following this, Coppelius vanished for a long time, but his eventual return ended in an explosion and

Hoffmann's illustration for 'The Sandman', 1815–16: Nathanael spies on his father and Coppelius.

the death of Nathanael's father. Now the trauma, supposedly healed by the passage of time, is reawakened by a visit to Nathanael by an Italian spectacle-seller called Coppola, whom the former thinks is the same person as Coppelius.

These childhood recollections need to be reported at length because the question of how to interpret them is central to the enigma of 'The Sandman'. Nathanael mistakenly sends this letter for Lothar to his fiancée, Clara, who is duly horrified. As a person of common sense, she is sure not only that Coppelius and Coppola cannot be the same person, but that Coppelius and Nathanael's father were engaged in nothing worse than alchemy, and that, if a dark, malevolent power exists, we can resist it by pursuing our lives in a spirit of cheerfulness. Nathanael does not like being lectured in this way, and the two gradually become estranged. Nathanael transfers his affections to Olimpia, supposedly the daughter of Spalanzani, the new professor of physics at his university. Everybody else is suspicious of Olimpia: her dance steps are curiously stiff, and her conversation is limited to 'Oh, oh!' She is in fact an automaton, but Nathanael discovers this only when, going to Spalanzani's house in order to propose to her, he hears a quarrel and discovers Spalanzani and Coppola fighting over Olimpia's lifeless body. Coppola is confirmed as Coppelius in disguise. He runs away, with Olimpia hanging over his shoulder. Spalanzani picks up the automaton's blood-stained eyes from the floor and throws them at Nathanael, who falls into a frenzy and is confined for some time in a madhouse. This sequence of events invites an interpretation that is both compelling and incredible. It would seem that when Nathanael spied on his father and Coppelius, they were not engaged in alchemy but trying to make an automaton, a simulacrum of a human being. They were rivals to God, whom Coppelius referred to as 'the Old Man'. There are many hints too that Nathanael's father was bound to Coppelius in a satanic or Faustian pact. The great difficulty of their work was getting the eyes right, which is why Coppelius threatened to use Nathanael's. Some twenty years later, Coppelius and Spalanzani have succeeded in producing an automaton, namely Olimpia. They want to use her to entrap Nathanael. A fire in Nathanael's house obliges him to move into lodgings opposite Spalanzani's home. With the aid of the (apparently magical) spyglass sold to him by Coppola, he peers at Olimpia through the window, and the more he gazes, the more her initially expressionless eyes seem to come to life. An unexplained quarrel between Spalanzani and Coppelius reveals the truth. Both accomplices vanish from the town.

Now, this narrative seems utterly at odds with common sense. It is more like a paranoid fantasy. Nathanael can certainly be said to be burdened by a childhood trauma which leads to an *idée fixe* such as Hoffmann found described in medical textbooks.[21] But suppose the story is a fantasy that corresponds to reality. Suppose there is really 'a well-calculated plan to involve Nathanael in Olimpia – an experiment in which, unknown to him, Nathanael has been chosen by Spalanzani and Coppola/Coppelius as their guinea-pig'.[22] That seems highly implausible, but the common-sense interpretation, which would explain Coppelius away as an alchemist and rationalize many other details, such as the unscrewing of the child's limbs, as mere illusions, is not adequate either. We are not entitled to reject textual details as illusory just because they do not fit our preferred interpretation.[23] And so, as an exploration of ambiguity, 'The Sandman' differs markedly from *The Golden Pot*. In the latter story, the two realities of Dresden and Atlantis are compatible, provided the reader has sufficient mental agility. In 'The Sandman', Nathanael's terror-haunted reality and Clara's sunny world are irreconcilable. You cannot have both, and the story draws no conclusion. Rather, we have here a feature that has recently been identified as characteristic of numerous Romantic works: the possibility of two interpretations that cannot exist at the same time – an analogy would be the drawings used by psychologists that can be variously perceived as depicting a duck or a rabbit, but not both.[24]

One might read 'The Sandman' as an exploration of the dangers of the poetic imagination. If Anselmus has a childlike poetic temperament, Nathanael's is morbid and obsessive. We are told that he used to write charming stories, but after Coppelius/Coppola re-enters his life he devotes his energies first to gloomy and boring poetry, then to a tale of terror that alarms even himself. When he insists on reading it aloud to Clara, she is horrified and urges him to throw it in the fire, whereupon Nathanael denounces her: 'You accursed lifeless automaton!' (*GP* 103). The irony is that he soon afterwards falls for the real automaton.

After the shocking revelation of Olimpia's true nature and Coppola's identity, Nathanael emerges from a stay in the madhouse, apparently cured, and he and Clara prepare to get married. Strolling through town, Clara proposes that they should climb the church tower. Once there, she draws attention to a little grey bush that seems to be moving towards them. Nathanael takes the spyglass from his pocket, looks through it at Clara, and is instantly overcome by madness. He is about to throw her off the tower, but her brother Lothar saves her. Just then, 'the gigantic figure of the advocate Coppelius, who had just arrived in the town' (*GP* 118), appears in the marketplace; on seeing him, Nathanael plunges to his death.

Is Clara unequivocally a force for good? Nathanael's tale of terror, which he earlier composed and shared with Clara, imagines

Coppelius throwing Clara's eyes at his breast, where they burn him. At the end, calm of a kind is restored: 'Nathanael gazes into Clara's eyes, but what looks at him from Clara's kindly eyes is death' (*GP* 102). Something sinister emanates even from her. It is Clara too who repeatedly prompts Nathanael's fits of madness: by wanting to climb the tower, and by noticing the grey bush that recalls Coppelius's bushy grey eyebrows. Even with his fiancée, Nathanael is not safe from dark forces.[25]

Was Nathanael doomed by external machinations or his own temperament, or both? One naturally seeks, perhaps futilely, for an explanation, and the most popular has been that put forward by Sigmund Freud in his essay 'The Uncanny' of 1919.[26] Freud, as usual, traces events and behaviours back to a parent, in this case the father. He argues that Nathanael's father-imago is split into the good father, who intercedes for the child's eyes, and the evil father, Coppelius, who threatens to tear them out. This splitting is repeated when Nathanael finds Spalanzani and Coppola fighting over Olimpia: Spalanzani represents the good father, Coppola again the evil one. The eyes are crucial because they symbolize testicles: the evil father is imagined as wishing to castrate the child. Nathanael's fixation on his father makes him incapable of love for a woman; he has, according to Freud, a narcissistic obsession with Olimpia because she is not a separate person but a doll onto whom he can project his own fantasies. Freud's interpretation is undeniably insightful, particularly in responding to Hoffmann's repeated representation of eyes as physical objects detached from the body to which they belong. Much subsequent commentary on 'The Sandman' has been devoted to elaborating or revising Freud's analysis of the tale. However, Freud treats the story as a case history rather than as a literary text.[27] He pays no attention to the narrator's reflections, which put the nature of reality into question. Under the influence of his own *idée fixe*, the supposed castration complex, Freud underrates the importance of vision in the story. Vision is repeatedly linked to forbidden knowledge. Surreptitious peeping and gazing – between curtains, through the spyglass – are recurrent motifs, culminating on the tower when Nathanael looks through the glass 'sideways' at

Clara (*GP* 117). In the spirit of Freud, one could speculate that the young Nathanael, in spying on his father and Coppelius as they made their automaton, was seeing what one is forbidden to see, namely the process of making a baby. This interpretation may gain support from Hoffmann's drawing, which depicts the father as effeminate, wearing a long robe and stooping, while Coppelius stands upright in a commanding, ultra-masculine posture.

The story also encodes worries about the mechanical enhancement of human capacity, represented by the sinister spyglass as well as the creation of an artificial human being. Hoffmann wrote this story in 1815, three years before Mary Shelley's *Frankenstein* was published. A year earlier, in 1814, Hoffmann explored the fascination and revulsion exerted by such contrivances in a fictional dialogue, 'Die Automate' ('The Automata'), originally published in *AMZ*. The speakers, Ferdinand and Ludwig, appear also in 'Der Dichter und der Komponist' ('The Poet and the Composer'), written in September and October 1813 and first published in the *AMZ* in December. Ludwig finds such things appalling:

> The very connection of a human being with dead figures that imitate humanity in their shape and movements and perform the same activities is for me oppressive, uncanny, indeed horrific. I can imagine that it must be possible, by means of a concealed internal mechanism, to make such figures dance skilfully and nimbly, and these might dance with human beings and turn and spin in all manner of moves, so that the living dancer would embrace his dead partner and swing round with her – could you endure the sight, even for a minute, without secret horror? (H II/1, 418)

The dialogue continues by contrasting the disagreeable mechanical music produced by a barrel organ with the attempts by true musicians to imitate and elaborate natural musical sounds. These, according to Ludwig, are themselves echoes of the time when primeval humanity lived 'in the original holy harmony with nature', a time recalled in the legend of the music of the spheres (H IV, 421).

Hoffmann places machinery and mechanical effects at the opposite extreme from nature. In 'The Sandman', written a year after this dialogue, Olimpia and her builders can be seen as the lowest point of a fallen world, and Nathanael as the possessor of a poetic talent that is subject to corruption.

The Devil's Elixirs

Needing money, Hoffmann wrote a thriller. *The Devil's Elixirs* is a *Schauerroman* (horror story or tale of terror), a genre that found innumerable readers in Germany around 1800. The popularity of the *Schauerroman* was heightened by anxiety among readers about semi-secret organizations existing in reality: the (harmless) Freemasons and the more sinister Illuminati, whose exposure in 1785 caused a panic out of all proportion to their numbers or powers; and a vast number of clubs, societies and reading circles. The former Illuminatus Adolph Freiherr von Knigge wrote in 1788: 'You will meet few people in any rank who have not, at least for a while, been members of such a secret brotherhood.'[28] A subgenre of popular fiction, the *Geheimbundroman* or 'secret society novel', catered to this fascination; Grosse's *The Genius*, which enthralled Hoffmann in 1795, is an example.

Hoffmann wrote the first half of the *Elixirs* over seven weeks in spring 1814. The pace of the story is as rapid as was its composition. The reader is drawn breathlessly along by the hero's adventures and by his barely controllable emotions. Although the hero is supposed to be recounting his experiences in retrospect, no subsequent reflection or explanation is allowed to disturb the onrush of inexplicable events or blunt their emotional impact. An early reader, the poet Heinrich Heine (1797–1856), wrote in 1822: '*The Devil's Elixirs* contains the most frightful and appalling things that the mind can think up . . . A student in Göttingen is said to have gone mad by reading it.'[29]

The novel's hero is a monk, christened Franz but renamed Medardus, who is tempted early by lust and pride. He is a remarkable preacher, but one day, while in full flow, he sees a tall,

Frontispiece to a 1920 edition of *Die Elixiere des Teufels* (The Devil's Elixirs), showing Medardus with the bottle.

gaunt, pale man staring at him and recognizes the figure as a painter whom he saw in his childhood decorating a chapel. In 'a mad fit of desperation', Medardus cries out: 'I AM SAINT ANTHONY!' (*DE* 28). This alludes to an elixir kept in the monastery as a precious relic. According to legend, this elixir is a wine with which the Devil tried to tempt St Anthony, who, instead of yielding, kept the bottle of elixir and bequeathed it to the Church. After his outburst, Medardus falls unconscious, and on his recovery he can no longer preach. Some impious worldly visitors whom Medardus is showing round the monastery insist on sampling St Anthony's wine and declare it is excellent 'Syracusan' (*DE* 30).[30] Later Medardus creeps down by himself and takes a mighty swig, with beneficial results for his eloquence – but he no longer preaches sincerely, being concerned only with his own pride.

Medardus's lust is aroused by glimpsing the concert master's sister half-dressed. Later it is revived by a veiled woman who approaches him to make her confession: she says that she is tormented by a sinful, forbidden love, then reveals that it is he, Medardus, whom she loves. Although he does not see her face, Medardus identifies her with St Rosalia, whose martyrdom is depicted in a painting nearby. Obsessed with the unknown woman, he howls madly with frustrated desire. When he has regained some self-control, Medardus is sent by the prior of the monastery, Leonardus, on a mission to Rome. He sets off, determined to track down his veiled lover, taking a good supply of the Devil's wine with him.

On his journey, among the mountains, Medardus sees a young man sitting on the edge of a precipice overlooking the Devil's Gorge. By addressing him too suddenly, Medardus inadvertently causes the stranger to fall off the cliff. It just so happens that this young man, Viktorin, is Medardus's double; Viktorin's servant, turning up, assumes that Medardus is his master. The family of Baron von F., whose castle is nearby, are expecting a priest, who has been sent for to treat the melancholy of the baron's son Hermogen. Medardus, recognized as the famous preacher, assumes this role, but also passes as Viktorin and continues the illicit liaison that Viktorin has been pursuing with the baroness, Euphemie. Thus Medardus has two identities: 'I am what I seem to be, yet do not seem to be what I am; even to myself I am an insoluble riddle, for my personality has been torn apart' (*DE* 54).

When the baron's daughter Aurelie arrives, Medardus recognizes her as the veiled woman of the confessional. Alongside his clandestine relationship with Euphemie, he feels truly drawn to Aurelie and considers how best to seduce her. Exploiting her devout character, he tries to transform religious devotion into sensual excitement, but his 'savage' embrace is rebuffed, and they are interrupted by the furious Hermogen. Euphemie, suspecting that Hermogen knows about their affair and will reveal it, orders Medardus to free her from her tedious elderly husband by murdering him; she also wants Medardus to seduce Aurelie, whose reserved manner annoys her. Medardus refuses both, poisons Euphemie before she can poison him, murders Hermogen and flees from the castle.

Thereafter Medardus's identity becomes yet more uncertain. He keeps encountering an insane monk who is his double, a terrifying, often violent being who cannot speak coherently. Much later we are asked to believe that this double is Viktorin, who survived his fall into the Devil's Gorge 'by some miracle' (*Zufall,* literally, 'accident'; *DE* 254), but this perfunctory explanation clarifies little. The double pursues Medardus, often claiming actually to be Medardus himself. Their identities seem to merge. The double, or Viktorin, not only haunts Medardus, even breaking through the floor of the prison cell where he is briefly confined (*DE* 161), but appears at two narrative climaxes. At the end of the chapter entitled 'The Turning Point', Medardus and Aurelie, after innumerable vicissitudes, are about to be married. As they wait at the door of the church, Medardus's double is carried past, on his way to be executed. He calls out to Medardus, who is seized by madness and reveals his true identity as the murderer of Aurelie's brother; he stabs Aurelie and runs off, forcing his way through the crowd with superhuman strength. No sooner has he reached the nearby forest and flung himself down to rest than the double appears and leaps on to his back.

They wrestle for what, to Medardus, seems like months, until he loses consciousness.

After many further adventures, Aurelie (since Medardus's blow was not fatal) is about to be received as a nun. Medardus is in the crowd watching the ceremony. Seeing that she is henceforth beyond his reach, Medardus feels an almost overwhelming temptation to intervene, but suppresses it by a mighty effort. This is the supreme triumph of his rational self over his unruly desires. Then, however, the double rushes in, wearing a tattered monastic robe, declares that Aurelie is his bride and stabs her. The crowd celebrate her as a martyr and identify her with the martyred St Rosalia. In her dying speech to Medardus, she repents of the guilty love she felt for him.

Both Medardus and Aurelie act parts already scripted for them by their family history. That history is revealed at intervals throughout the novel, most fully by a manuscript written by their ancestor, a Renaissance painter called Francesco. Francesco, like his descendant Medardus, was filled with pride and lust. Commissioned to paint St Rosalia, he modelled her on a portrait of Venus, thereby mingling the sacred with the profane. Francesco then had an affair with a beautiful woman who resembled his Venus but was rumoured to be an emissary of the Devil. Francesco was placed under a curse: he could not die until his family was extinct. His descendants repeatedly committed rape, murder and blasphemy. The extremely complicated family tree ends with the half-brothers Franz, alias Medardus, and Viktorin; the unscrupulous Euphemie, bedmate of Viktorin and Medardus and poisoned by the latter, was Medardus's half-sister; Aurelie and Medardus have the same grandfather.[31] The painter is therefore intent on preventing these two from marrying, and he is successful.

How are we to interpret Medardus's story? It offers a field day to the psychoanalyst. The painter who interrupts Medardus's eloquence can be read as the super-ego; the violent, inarticulate double as the id. Medardus's desire for Aurelie is really a desire for his mother's body, hence a furious passion that is also taboo. Characters embody different aspects of Medardus: Aurelie and Euphemie 'can be seen as female constituents of Medardus's psyche, reflecting back aspects of himself'.[32] Such readings go back to Freud, who writes briefly about *The Devil's Elixirs* in 'The Uncanny', and they can be convincing and even illuminating on their own terms.[33] Often, though, they seem gratuitous. Why does Medardus's obsession with Aurelie have to spring from a mother-fixation?

Hoffmann's medical reading, and indeed his own experience, gave him a rich store of psychological concepts, which in turn are interwoven with this novel's problematic religious discourse. From his diaries we can see that Hoffmann thought a great deal about madness (an example is 6 January 1811) and readily imagined his own personality as multiple: 'Strange idea at the ball . . . I imagine myself through a multiplying glass – all the figures moving around me are versions of myself [*Ichs*]' (6 November 1809). His reading told him much about *idées fixes*, obsessions sometimes developing into madness.[34] His own attachment to Julia Marc was an *idée fixe*. The mutual attraction between Aurelie and Medardus, which drives Aurelie to confess her love for him, builds on the concept of magnetic rapport. The aggression towards Aurelie that accompanies Medardus's raging desire for her corresponds to the ambivalence noted sombrely by G. H. Schubert: 'even in the natural state sensual desire [*Wollust*] is only a mask concealing a pleasure in destruction and murder.'[35] And it was a contemporary commonplace that the solitude and monotony of monastic life conduced to insanity. However, while Hoffmann starts from the ideas of his time, he develops them in original ways. He represents personality not only as multiple but as fluid: Medardus and his double merge into each other. And he describes many elaborate dreams that cannot always be distinguished from waking experience.[36]

How seriously are we to take the novel's religious framework? Catholic rituals and monastic seclusion often appeared in horror fiction, especially that written by and for Protestants. Some of the novel's clerical figures, the weak and worldly pope (probably based on Pius VI, who reigned 1775–99) and the murderous Dominicans who assemble in underground vaults, belong to such fiction. However, the wise and humane Leonardus, prior of Medardus's Capuchin monastery, represents the Catholic Enlightenment.

Widely travelled and master of several languages, he combines the spirit of antiquity with the 'dark mysticism of Christianity' (*DE* 16). He does not like talking about miracles and shows scepticism when Medardus tells how as a child he was visited by St Joseph and the child Jesus, so that Medardus, already tending towards fanaticism, thinks him a 'secret sceptic' (*DE* 19). The thrilling spiritual drama that Medardus enacts, from blasphemous sin to death in the odour of sanctity, has above all an aesthetic appeal. It resembles the play by Calderón, *The Devotion of the Cross*, which Hoffmann enthusiastically staged in Bamberg and in which the incestuous couple are redeemed, one clinging to the cross and the other welcoming her in heaven.[37]

The force that drives Medardus to salvation is ambiguously called *Macht* (power) or *Verhängnis* (destiny, with negative implications). When the penitent Medardus finally confesses his sins to Leonardus, he says he is being punished by 'the eternal inscrutable power' (H II/2, 325: *der ewigen unerforschlichen Macht*, misleadingly translated as 'Heaven', *DE* 252).[38] Leonardus affirms that evil is necessary for good to emerge: 'the principle of moral goodness presupposes the test of evil' (*DE* 260). For most of the text, however, it seems that an external power colludes with Medardus's sinful impulses to draw him further into crime. This ambiguity is characteristic of much German literature around 1800. In Schiller's tragedy *Wallenstein* (completed in 1799), although all the characters are nominally Christians, they talk in the pre-Christian language of 'fate', 'destiny' and 'dark powers'. In Tieck's novella *Der blonde Eckbert* (Fair-Haired Eckbert, 1797) the protagonist is drawn by a mysterious vengeful force into murder, madness and incest. The popular genre of 'fate tragedy', such as Zacharias Werner's *Der 24. Februar* (The 24th of February, 1810), similarly shows characters at the mercy of inexplicable compulsion. Medardus's will is repeatedly taken over by an alien force that tells him what to say in difficult situations and gives him an extraordinary run of luck in gambling.

The Devil's Elixirs and 'The Sandman' are the acknowledged high points of a phase in Hoffmann's writing, 1814–17, dominated by terror and the supernatural. 'The Sandman' sets the tone for the collection *Nachtstücke* (Night-Pieces), which Hoffmann published in two volumes in 1816 and 1817. It has a gruesome but cruder companion piece in 'Ignaz Denner', in which an honest forester called Andres is drawn into the clutches of the title figure, a bandit, and of the latter's father, Dr Trabacchio, who is in league with the Devil or may even be the Devil himself. Although *Night-Pieces* includes some mysterious but not terrifying tales, it gave Hoffmann a lasting but misleading reputation as a writer only of horror stories. Thus Heine claimed that Hoffmann's 'works are nothing but a terrible cry of anguish in twenty volumes'.[39] But Heine also acknowledged that 'Hoffmann, with all his bizarre caricatures, always clung firmly to earthly reality.'[40] This duality – flights of fantasy that always retain a link to familiar reality, and depend on the familiar to carry conviction – would not only characterize the fiction that Hoffmann, in great demand from magazine editors, produced prolifically after his return to Berlin, but be fundamental to the poetics of fiction that he elaborated.

3

Hoffmann the Storyteller

The Hoffmanns arrived in Berlin in September 1814. After eight months in temporary accommodation, they moved into a flat overlooking the Gendarmenmarkt in the city centre. It is from this flat that the 'cousin' in the late story 'Des Vetters Eckfenster' ('My Cousin's Corner Window', 1822) observes the bustle of the market, and the flat and its surroundings are also the subject of a highly elaborate drawing, made on 18 July 1815, that shows to the full Hoffmann's talent as a caricaturist. The passers-by include well-known literary figures along with Epimenides, 'Nemo' (that is, Nobody) and an ostrich.[1]

On 1 October 1814 Hoffmann reluctantly but resolutely re-entered the state's legal service. He was attached to the Supreme Court (Kammergericht), initially with only occasional payment. He was worried that his legal knowledge might be rusty and that he might be caught out in a mistake. Nevertheless, he applied himself with success. In June 1815 he obtained a salaried post and in April 1816 he was given the title and position of councillor (*Rat*) at the Supreme Court. He still hoped to resume a career in music as a Kapellmeister (musical director) in the Berlin theatre, as he wrote to Hippel (28 April 1815):

> I cannot simply give up the arts, and if I did not have to provide for a beloved wife and give her a comfortable situation after all she has endured with me, I would sooner go back to being a musical schoolmaster than be confined in the legal treadmill.

The house that Hoffmann lived in between 1815 and 1822 at Charlottenstraße 39, corner Taubenstraße 31, photograph dated 1914.

To support himself and Mischa, Hoffmann had to combine legal work with the writing of fiction. The first two volumes of *Fantasy-Pieces* had aroused interest that was enormously heightened by the publication of *The Golden Pot* in November 1814. Soon, requests for stories poured in from the editors of magazines and anthologies. To meet the demand, Hoffmann sometimes had to literally combine law and literature. He wrote the scene from 'The Sandman' in which Coppelius threatens the child Nathanael during a session of the Supreme Court. One of his letters to Kunz is written from the court, where he is sitting next to the presiding judge, screened by a pile of documents (24 May 1815).

Hoffmann's literary reputation made Berlin writers curious to meet him. His friend Hitzig, who had lived in Berlin for several years working as a lawyer and a bookseller, arranged a dinner on 27 September 1814 to introduce Hoffmann to a number of Berlin-based writers. These included two prominent Romantic authors: Ludwig Tieck and Friedrich, Baron de la Motte Fouqué (1777–1843). Hoffmann admired such witty metatheatrical comedies as Tieck's *Der gestiefelte Kater* (Puss in Boots, 1797), in which an audience appears on stage and comments on the play being performed in front of it, but as Tieck soon afterwards moved to Dresden, they had no further contact. Fouqué on the other hand became a friend and collaborator, though the friendship later cooled when Hoffmann's works became more popular than Fouqué's. Fouqué was the author of the fairy-tale novella *Undine* (1811) and had already, at Hoffmann's request, adapted it as an opera with music by Hoffmann. He was famous for his dramas and novels based on Germanic myths (anticipating Wagner), and Hoffmann was enthusiastic about his novel *Der Zauberring* (The Magic Ring, 1812; letter to Hitzig, 15 August 1812). The contact between Hoffmann in Bamberg and Fouqué in Berlin had been mediated by Hitzig; the two were now meeting for the first time. Also present was Adelbert von Chamisso (1781–1838), an adoptive German born in France; his best-known story, *Peter Schlemihls wundersame Geschichte* (The Wondrous Tale of Peter Schlemihl, 1814), about a man who sells his shadow, so appealed to Hoffmann that he introduced Schlemihl into the fourth volume of *Fantasy-Pieces* (published in 1815) alongside the man who gives away his mirror-image. Chamisso, a scientist, left Berlin in 1815

E.T.A. Hoffmann, *Schlemihl Sails to the North Pole (Expedition of Count Rumyantsev)*, 1816, caricature showing Hoffmann's friend Adelbert von Chamisso, on his voyage round the world, greeting the North Pole.

for a three-year voyage of exploration on the Russian ship *Rurik*. He would later provide Hoffmann with geographical and entomological information for the little story 'Haimatochare' (1819), set in Hawaii.

What did the other diners make of Hoffmann? Tieck recalled: 'Hoffmann had a remarkable appearance, a restless little man with exceptionally mobile features and piercing eyes. There was something uncanny about him' (A 282). Contemporaries agree on Hoffmann's unusually small stature and his restless activity. Some recall his tiny, delicate hands (A 377) and glittering, falcon-like eyes (A 370). He did not like tea parties, because there he could not dominate the conversation (A 370). He could not stand being bored and would respond to others either with silence or with sarcasm. Among a circle of drinking companions, however, he would hold everyone spellbound by his flow of brilliant, often biting wit. Some people, like Tieck, were uneasy in his presence, perhaps sensing his unresolved inner conflicts, to which the writer Fanny Tarnow (1779–1862) referred when speaking of his 'Zerrissenheit' (inner division; A 418). He liked uncomfortable practical jokes. Once, he persuaded all the company after dinner to cover their heads with white napkins, extinguished the lights and set light to some brandy so that the group looked like an assembly of ghosts (A 404). Another time he disconcerted a guest, the Danish poet Adam Oehlenschläger (1779–1850), by producing a puppet with the head of a devil; apparently he had a cupboard full of such toys (A 417).

Two other Berlin friends deserve mention. One was David Koreff (1783–1851), a physician who shared Hoffmann's interest in magnetism and held a professorship of animal magnetism at the University of Berlin. Koreff was personal physician to Prince Hardenberg, the Prussian chancellor, but his liberal political views brought him into disfavour and from 1822 onwards he lived in Paris. The other was the famous actor Ludwig Devrient (1784–1832), one of only a handful of people with whom Hoffmann shared the intimate pronoun *du*. Although Devrient excelled in the tragic roles of King Lear and Karl Moor (from Schiller's *The Robbers*), he also had a gift for comedy, shown in his appearance as Falstaff and in many ephemeral plays.

Hermann Kramer, *E.T.A. Hoffmann and Ludwig Devrient in the Lutter & Wegner Wine Tavern*, 1843, oil on canvas.

Once Hoffmann was settled in Berlin, his daily routine, according to Hitzig, was as follows: on Monday and Thursday mornings he would attend sessions of the Supreme Court, while on other mornings he would work at home; in the afternoons he would take a nap and, in summer, go for a walk. It is not clear when he wrote his stories, especially as most of them, far from being dashed off hastily, are intricately constructed and sometimes, especially those with a historical basis such as the novella 'Das Fräulein von Scuderi' ('Mademoiselle de Scudery', 1820), rest on extensive research. He cannot have been out every night, but he clearly liked to spend his evenings amid a circle of friends, usually in Lutter & Wegner's wine cellar near his home on the Gendarmenmarkt. He would often stay out drinking late, sometimes until morning.

Drinking is overwhelmingly present in Hoffmann's life, and prominent in his fiction. His favourite wine was Chambertin, a full-bodied red Burgundy (letter to Kunz, 8 September 1813). On his death he owed 1,116 Reichsthaler for drinks; as a comparison, his annual salary in 1815 amounted to 800 Reichsthaler.[2] Devrient too drank heavily, despite his wife's efforts to restrain him. Once, to prove how sluggish Berlin workmen were, he wagered that he could empty a bottle of champagne in less time than a mason would need to take a pinch of snuff; he won his bet (A 443). Hoffmann was blamed for shortening Devrient's life by irresponsibly encouraging his drinking.

Was Hoffmann an alcoholic? Victoria Dutchman-Smith, who has investigated this question, finds 'alcoholism' too inexact a concept to be useful.[3] Certainly Hoffmann drank a great deal. But alcohol seems to have been a stimulus for him, not a depressant. This is the function, for example, of the arrack that the archivist presses on the narrator at the end of *The Golden Pot*: it affords him a vision of the happy life that Anselmus and Serpentina are leading in Atlantis. One can hardly doubt, however, that his heavy alcohol consumption helped to shorten Hoffmann's life, along with the pressures of legal work, which he performed impeccably, and of fulfilling editors' demands for stories. Probably a life lived with such intensity could not have been long in any case: Hoffmann seems to have been, in John Dryden's lines, 'A fiery Soul, which working out its way,/ Fretted the Pigmy Body to decay.'[4]

Hoffmann's Poetics

Having published many stories in periodicals, Hoffmann had them reprinted with additions in two collections, *Night-Pieces* and

The Serapion Brethren. The *Night-Pieces* include some of the 'tales of terror', notably 'The Sandman', which gained Hoffmann a one-sided reputation as a horror writer and the sobriquet 'Gespenster-Hoffmann' ('Ghosts Hoffmann'). Along with *The Devil's Elixirs*, they come from the period 1814 to 1817, during which 'we see Hoffmann increasingly haunted by satanic figures of various kinds.'[5]

The stories collected in *The Serapion Brethren* are more varied and less grim. Not all of them even imply the supernatural. They are connected by a framework in which four, later six, friends (Theodor, Lothar, Ottmar and Cyprian, joined by Vincenz and Sylvester) meet regularly to tell each other stories and discuss them. The framing device goes back to Boccaccio's *Decameron* (*c.* 1350) and Chaucer's *Canterbury Tales* (*c.* 1387–1400). Recent examples were Goethe's *Unterhaltungen deutscher Ausgewanderten* (Conversations among German Emigrants, 1795), in which aristocrats forced to flee from the French invasion of the Rhineland use their enforced leisure to exchange stories, and – particularly mentioned by Hoffmann – *Phantasus* (1812–17), in which Tieck assembled his previously published stories. Hoffmann and some Berlin friends founded a storytelling club, initially called the Seraphinenorden (Order of St Seraphina). The club broke up when Chamisso, one of its members, left for his three-year voyage round the world, and was re-established as the Serapion Brotherhood (Serapionsbrüder) on 14 November 1818, because that date, as Mischa showed them from a Catholic calendar, was the day commemorating St Serapion. It provided Hoffmann with a fictional framework for his stories. Some of the narrators of his tales can be loosely identified with Hoffmann and his friends: thus Cyprian resembles Hoffmann, Vincenz is modelled on Koreff. But the narrators are not character portraits; rather they represent different standpoints in the discussions that link the stories.

Near the beginning of *The Serapion Brethren*, Cyprian tells how during his residence in 'B.' (Bamberg) he encountered in a secluded spot near the town a hermit in a monk's habit. This person, he learned, was Count P., who had been cured of violent insanity in the clinic of Dr S. (Hoffmann's friend Speyer) but persisted in the fixed idea that he was none other than Serapion, who suffered martyrdom under Emperor Decius (r. 249–51 CE), and was now living in the Egyptian desert. When Cyprian tried to persuade the hermit that he was deluded, and that the city visible in the distance was not Alexandria but Bamberg, the hermit rebuffed him with specious but unanswerable reasoning. Discussing his case, the friends arrive at the view that the self-styled Serapion was a true poet, but lacked the one thing needful – a grounding in reality:

> Poor Serapion, what was your madness but the fact that some hostile star had robbed you of the perception of the duality [*Duplizität*] that alone determines all our earthly being. An inner world does exist, as does the spiritual power to behold it in full clarity, in the most perfect radiance of the most active life; but our earthly lot is such that the external world in which we are enclosed serves as the lever to set that power in motion. Internal phenomena are embodied in the circle that external phenomena form around us, and which the spirit can transcend only in dark, mysterious intuitions that never shape themselves into a distinct image. But you, O my hermit, did not acknowledge the external world, you did not see the concealed lever, the force operating on your internal power. (H IV, 68)

There are two ways of escaping from this duality that governs our existence. One can take refuge in madness, like Serapion, or remain satisfied with a one-dimensional view of the world, like the townswoman in *The Golden Pot* who sees Anselmus embracing a tree and concludes: 'That gentleman doesn't seem to be right in the head!' (*GP* 7). Escape may be tempting, for the awareness of being trapped in a prosaic reality can be frustrating and painful – as it is for Lindhorst, exiled from Atlantis, and for Kreisler, who yearns for the transcendent world of music. But this duality is also the source of the humour that provides not just the content but the structure of much of Hoffmann's work.[6]

Since they recognize Serapion as a genuine poet, the four friends adopt him as their patron saint. They resolve that whatever stories they compose must not be mere arbitrary and bodiless fantasies: 'Let everyone examine whether he has really beheld what he means to relate, before he ventures to put it into words' (H IV, 69). That does not mean that the content of the stories must be taken from experience, but that it must be imagined concretely and in detail. As Theodor puts it later, the poet may ascend on a ladder from earth to heaven, but the ladder must be firmly based on the ground (H IV, 721). It is clear from the context that Theodor has in mind the eighteenth-century fashion for Oriental tales (for example, Christoph Martin Wieland's *Dschinnistan* of 1786–9), which suffered because their authors, unlike the author of the *Thousand and One Nights*, were not based in the realities inhabited by the dervishes, merchants, porters, tailors and so forth who populate the *Nights*. The friends call their artistic theory 'the Serapiontic principle' (H IV, 70).[7]

The 'Serapiontic principle' needs to be set alongside another that is equally crucial for Hoffmann's poetics. In 'The Sandman', after presenting the three letters with which the story begins, the narrator reflects on the difficulty of conveying his inner vision. He compares himself to a painter who begins with a sketch, then goes on 'adding ever brighter colours until the swirling throng of multifarious figures seized hold of your friends' imagination' (*GP* 98). So,

> I may, like a good portraitist, succeed in depicting some figures so that you find them good likenesses even without knowing the originals; indeed, you may feel as though you had often seen these persons with your very own eyes. Thus, O my reader, you may come to believe that nothing can be stranger or weirder than real life, and that the poet can do no more than capture the strangeness of reality, like the dim reflection in a dull mirror. (*GP* 98–9)

Here, in contrast to *The Serapion Brethren*, the emphasis is placed more on the poet's imagination than on the earthly reality that sustains it. Nevertheless, the interaction between the two is still essential. Here again the poet is not copying reality but taking colours from reality in order to add vividness and shape to his amorphous inner vision. The poet's business is not to inform us about the external world we already inhabit – the 'real world' perceived by unimaginative philistines – but to introduce us to a strange and weird reality in which the 'real world' is suffused by the poet's imagination.

Hoffmann's aesthetics repeatedly adumbrate a transcendent realm of which we can only have tantalizing intuitions. Can the poet ever go further and convey distinctly, not just as an obscure intuition, a reality transcending both inner and outer experience? Looking back to Hoffmann's musical criticism, he finds in music 'an unknown realm, a world quite separate from the outer sensual world', conveying 'an inexpressible longing' (C 96). But not only is the longing 'inexpressible' in words, its object is unknowable, always retreating beyond the horizon of possible experience. Hoffmann perhaps conveys this transcendent realm only in the myths that are interwoven into three of his greatest stories, *The Golden Pot, Princess Brambilla* and *Master Flea*. In *The Golden Pot* Anselmus overcomes the conflict between the real world of Dresden and his equally real poetic imagination by escaping with Serpentina into the magical realm of Atlantis. This can be seen as Hoffmann's version of a narrative pattern favoured in Romantic literature and thought, whereby contraries are ultimately reconciled in a higher synthesis.[8]

Hoffmann was writing in the wake of the philosophical revolution initiated by Kant, who argued that our knowledge of the world is conditioned by the structure of our minds and their interaction with the experience provided by our senses. The real character of the world, the *Ding an sich* (thing-in-itself), is permanently unknowable. Hoffmann, however, did not read much philosophy, apart from ploughing through Schelling's *On the World Soul*. Rather than trying to map his aesthetic ideas in detail onto post-Kantian idealism, it may be more pertinent to remember his enthusiasm for the Catholic dramas of Calderón, in which the transcendent is given definite concrete embodiment: 'it is in the spirit of Catholicism to draw on the senses when symbolically representing that which lies beyond the senses.'[9]

Frame and Story: Serapion and Krespel

Although the stories in *The Serapion Brethren* work perfectly as self-contained narratives, they gain something by being located in a larger cycle of tales accompanied by discussion. An example is the story to which Hoffmann did not give a title, but which is generally known as 'Rat Krespel' ('Krespel the Councillor'). It is inserted into the discussion that follows Cyprian's account of his acquaintance with Serapion. Cyprian defends his liking for the company of lunatics on the grounds that in such people nature reveals her 'terrifying depths' (H IV, 37). Theodor objects that though Serapion was harmless and even happy, madness is always an alarming and dangerous subject. Ottmar professes to avoid lunatics like the plague. Theodor rebukes this excessive reaction and undertakes to tell a story that will provide a transition from madness via melancholy to healthy good sense. He recounts the life of somebody who was eccentric but, unlike Serapion, by no means insane. Theodor's story concerns Krespel, who is a distinguished lawyer and successful diplomat yet highly eccentric in his personal life.[10] His movements are so stiff and jerky that he seems constantly about to bump into something or do damage, yet he never does. He directs the building of his house in a strange way: the masons are to raise the walls until Krespel tells them to stop; he orders windows to be inserted in unexpected places, so that the completed house looks bizarre, yet inside it is perfectly comfortable. This discrepancy between inside and outside is also characteristic of Krespel. His behaviour is extraordinary, yet has a strange logic to it.

Central to Krespel's life is his relationship with his daughter Antonie. The story emerges gradually. He met and married her mother, Angela, a gifted singer, in Italy, but the marriage broke up after a violent quarrel in which she smashed his violin and he threw her out of a (fortunately ground-floor) window. Krespel returned to Germany and lived 'like a hermit' (*Tales* 164). Angela let Krespel know that she had given birth to their daughter, but Krespel made no attempt at reconciliation. He did not meet Antonie until her mother's death, by which time Antonie was grown up and engaged to marry a young composer, known as B. Her father was enthralled by the young woman's beauty and her marvellous singing voice, but when she sang he claimed to perceive an unhealthy flush, which a physician told him indicated 'an organic defect in her chest' (*Tales*, 180); if she went on singing, she would die within six months. Krespel therefore forbade Antonie to sing or to marry, since he feared her husband would persuade her to sing. All young men who show an interest in her, including Theodor, are brusquely ejected from the house; only B., whose music Krespel admires, is an exception.

The violin acquires crucial symbolic significance. Krespel's main occupation is buying old violins, taking them to pieces and building new ones from their parts. There is one particularly fine violin with which Antonie identifies, so that she persuades him not to destroy it. But on Antonie's death, which comes about mysteriously, Krespel claims that the violin spontaneously shattered. On the night of her passing Krespel had a dream in which Antonie sang and B. accompanied her on the piano; when he woke, he found Antonie lying dead, with an expression of bliss on her face. Thereafter,

Councillor Krespel kneeling beside the corpse of his daughter Antonie, scene from the premiere of Offenbach's *Les Contes d'Hoffmann* (1881).

Krespel not only resolves to no longer make violins, but rejoices as though released from a painful obsession.

This story is not a puzzle to be solved, but an often oblique enactment of diverse and painful emotions. Krespel's aggressiveness accompanies an exceptional sensitivity. He is said to lack the protective shell that shelters most people, so that he displays the emotions that the rest of us conceal, like certain insects whose skin is so thin that the motion of their muscles is visible.[11] 'What with us remains thought, becomes with Krespel – deed. The mad gestures and convulsive leaps are an acting out of the bitterness he feels within' (*Tales* 173), Hoffmann writes. Krespel's behaviour to others is extreme: he throws his wife out of the window and resolves never to see her again, and he will not allow his beloved daughter to leave his house. It has been plausibly suggested that Antonie's 'organic defect' is invented by Krespel in order to keep undisputed possession of her. Her illness clearly distresses him, yet his reaction after her death is grotesquely inappropriate.[12] Hoffmann has written a psychological study that points towards murky emotional depths. His story is moreover told in a non-linear fashion (obscured in the above summary), which imposes a lot of work on the reader.

The story is badly received by Lothar, who finds Krespel a much more disturbing figure than Serapion and accuses Theodor of distorting events to make them more wondrous. Theodor protests that he is not making up fiction but recounting real events that he witnessed. If Lothar finds the tales exaggerated and improbable, he should remember that 'what really happens is almost always the most improbable thing' (H IV, 65). This is a standard defence of 'improbable' events in fiction, formulated by the seventeenth-century French critic Nicolas Boileau-Despréaux, in his *L'Art poétique* (1674): 'The True may sometimes not be probable.'[13] Hoffmann, who admired the fiction of Heinrich von Kleist, certainly knew the passage in the latter's story *Michael Kohlhaas* (1810), in which the narrator justifies a coincidence by asserting that 'probability and reality do not always coincide.'[14] Lothar also complains that as the story, owing to its intricate non-linear structure, ends with Antonie's death, it lacks a comforting resolution. Theodor obliquely answers this charge much later in the collection. Another story he recounts, 'The Automata', ends without explaining how the titular automaton, a machine shaped like a Turk, is able to answer the questions put to it. Theodor replies that if the story is a fragment, that itself has value in stimulating the reader's imagination, and he cites Goethe as an exemplar: 'A fragmentary story has often penetrated deep into my soul and provided me with lasting enjoyment by making my imagination spread its wings. Who didn't feel this with Goethe's *Nut-Brown Girl*?' (H IV, 428).[15] The complete text of *The Serapion Brethren* provides not only stories but reflections on the stories. It can be read not only as a collection of tales, but as a poetics of fiction illustrated by narratives.

Hoffmann's tales – in the *Night-Pieces, The Serapion Brethren* and the uncollected later stories – are so numerous and so various that I will discuss in detail only a small number of acknowledged masterpieces. To classify them in groups by genre or theme has only limited value, since genres tend to overlap. Tales of terror predominate in the *Night-Pieces*, but *The Serapion Brethren* also includes such frightening stories as 'Der unheimliche Gast ('The Uncanny Guest') and an untitled narrative about vampires (H IV, 1119–34). And, as we shall see, there are elements of terror also in such children's fairy tales as 'Nussknacker und Mausekönig' ('The Nutcracker and the Mouse-King').

One of the *Night-Pieces*, the story entitled 'The Entail', illustrates the coexistence in Hoffmann's work of rational, enlightened consciousness (indicated by the legal term in the title) and an openness to the supernatural. In a remote, desolate landscape that anticipates Edgar Allan Poe's (1809–1849) short supernatural horror story 'The Fall of the House of Usher', originally published in 1839, the narrator, Theodor, and his uncle, a lawyer, are visiting the Baron von R. on legal business. During the night they hear sinister groans. The next day the uncle insists that he and Theodor must leave at once. Some months later, he tells Theodor the story of the R. family, a complicated narrative involving hidden treasure, murder and a vengeful ghost. The ghost is that of an old servant named Daniel, whom the uncle and nephew heard groaning during their stay at the castle. Daniel plays a dual role. He provides a case of documents that help the uncle to establish the true heir to the estate. But he also, first as a living man and later as a ghost, contrives the deaths of family members and brings about the extinction of the R. family. The uncle also has a dual role. Far from denying the supernatural, he confronts Daniel's ghost and commands it to seek God's mercy. His Christian convictions do not prevent him from ascribing the family's fate to 'the evil power which resides in that place' (*Tales* 251).[16] But he also engages in laborious archival research to confirm the truth of the documents that Daniel has brought to light. He inhabits both worlds, the supernatural and the rational, and helps the latter to triumph. Once the family is extinct, the ruins of the castle are used by the state to build a lighthouse – a symbol of enlightenment.

The Artist as Criminal: 'The Jesuit Church in G–' and 'Mademoiselle de Scudery'

The story 'The Jesuit Church in G–' is told by the travelling enthusiast who features in other Hoffmann stories, such as 'Don Juan', and set in Glogau, where Hoffmann himself stayed in 1796–8. The narrator is obliged to spend several days there while his carriage is being repaired. He encounters two contrasting figures: Professor Walther of the Jesuit college, a worldly materialist who does not share the enthusiast's admiration for the supra-sensual spirit of Gothic architecture, 'that sacred dignity, that lofty majesty of the Gothic building striving heavenwards' (H III, 111), and Berthold, a painter hired to redecorate the church with classical scenes taken from earthly life, a task the enthusiast helps with. Walther asserts that although we may have a heavenly home, so long as we are alive our kingdom is of this world (cynically reversing Jesus' words at John 18:36: 'My kingdom is not of this world'). In extreme contrast to the Professor, Berthold thinks that the artist should strive for 'the highest in divine Nature, the Promethean spark in humanity' (H IV, 117). Berthold is a disturbing figure: he works by torchlight, as though shunning daylight, and seems weighed down by guilt for a crime to which he refers enigmatically.

To elucidate the mystery, the professor shows the narrator a manuscript, in which a former student recorded Berthold's account of his life. Early in his career Berthold attempted landscape and history painting, but after glimpsing a beautiful woman, Princess Angiola, who seemed to embody his ideal, he took to idealized portraits in the manner of Raphael. Amid the upheavals of the French occupation of Naples in 1797–8, he saved Angiola's life and took her to Germany. When commissioned to paint the Virgin, he found he could only paint Angiola. The beauty of the real woman distracted him from imagining and depicting ideal beauty. He cursed and kicked her; she and their child disappeared. Although their fate is unknown, nobody believes that Berthold murdered them, nor knows why he accuses himself of a crime. Berthold fell gravely ill, and on recovering, scraped a living as an itinerant painter. After the enthusiast has left Glogau, he learns from Professor Walther that Berthold completed the painting, which is much admired, but then vanished, and is thought to have killed himself (H III, 140).

The story leaves many questions unanswered. Berthold is associated with Prometheus, who in Greek mythology stole fire from the gods to benefit humankind. His supposed crime recalls that of the painter in *The Devil's Elixirs* who confused the real beauty of his mistress with the ideal beauty of St Rosalia. Could it be that the artist is by nature sacrilegious, either in revealing divine mysteries to the world or in obscuring the ideal by depicting the empirical world? If so, Berthold implicitly rejects the Serapiontic principle that the artist's ideal needs to be embodied in forms taken from the world around him.

'Mademoiselle de Scudery', set in late seventeenth-century Paris, features two artists. One, named in the title, is a historical figure, the novelist and salon hostess Madeleine de Scudéry (1608–1701); the other is an invented figure, the goldsmith René Cardillac. Scudery, a benevolent character, inhabits a shallow courtly milieu where art is only a parlour game; Cardillac is a dedicated artist but also a deeply sinister figure.

The initial mystery is twofold. Paris, already terrorized by a wave of poisonings, now suffers a series of unexplained murders, all committed at night, of men carrying jewels to their lovers.[17] There is also a puzzle concerning Cardillac, who is always inexplicably reluctant to part with the jewels he has made into necklaces. The solution is provided by his apprentice Olivier, who sees Cardillac committing a murder and then eluding pursuit by vanishing into a hidden doorway. Olivier tries in vain to warn Scudery against owning jewellery made by Cardillac. Cardillac is found murdered; Olivier is arrested and threatened with torture. He manages to secure an interview with Scudery, who knew him as a child, and tells her his story. Being in love with Cardillac's daughter, he continued working with Cardillac despite being aware that it was Cardillac who was committing the murders. Cardillac one day confided his story. When his mother was pregnant with him, she was attracted by a cavalier, especially by his jewels. The two embraced, but as his mother was grasping the cavalier's chain, he suddenly died and fell on top of her. She had to call for help to extricate herself. Cardillac invokes the long-standing theory that strong impressions felt by a pregnant woman can have lasting influence on her child. To this Cardillac attributes not only his love of jewels but his desire to murder their wearers. What he does not say, however, is that his destined victims are specifically young men planning to offer jewels to their lovers.

'Mademoiselle de Scudery' has sometimes been claimed as the first detective story, anticipating by some twenty years Edgar Allan Poe's 'The Murders in the Rue Morgue' (1841). However, in contrast to Poe's detective Dupin, Scudery does not actually solve the crime; she hears Olivier's report of Cardillac's confession and, through her connections at court, is able to persuade the king of Olivier's innocence. As an artist fully integrated into society, she contrasts sharply with Cardillac. His eccentricity turns out to spring from a murderous obsession. Cardillac has a double character that almost makes him a Jekyll and Hyde figure. By day a respected artist, at night he roams the streets committing acts of violence.

In this crime story, the real mystery is not 'who' but 'why'. Cardillac's confession does not fully explain his crimes. If taken at face value, it reveals the psychology of a murderer impelled either by fate or by a strange quirk, as was often attested in the medical literature that Hoffmann knew. But it is rendered uncertain by being located at several narrative removes. Whoever told Cardillac this story, it was not his mother.[18] Cardillac tells the story to Olivier, who tells it to Scudery; it cannot be verified. What matters is that Cardillac believes it and uses it to exonerate himself by claiming that he was born under an 'evil star' (*Tales* 63). The narrator describes Cardillac as 'one of the most artistically gifted and at the same time strangest men of his age' (*Tales* 34). This recalls Kleist's *Michael Kohlhaas*, whose protagonist is introduced as 'one of the most honourable as well as one of the most terrible men of his age'. Both Kohlhaas and Cardillac are obsessed: Kohlhaas with justice – 'But his sense of justice made him a robber and a murderer' – and Cardillac with sexual delinquency.[19] The men he murders as they carry jewels to their lovers are new versions of the cavalier who seduced his mother. As John M. Ellis writes, 'Both Cardillac and Kohlhaas become megalomaniac avenging angels correcting the vices of the world.'[20] Cardillac's fanaticism about virtue echoes the determination of the Paris police, presented at some length in the story, to eradicate crime by spreading terror.

Märchen

The term 'fairy tale' is probably unavoidable, but certainly misleading, as a translation of the German word *Märchen*, which makes one think first of the folktales collected (and often adapted) by the brothers Jacob and Wilhelm Grimm in the early 1800s. These popular stories or folktales (*Volksmärchen*), however, existed alongside the *Kunstmärchen* (literary folktale), 'a tale embodying folk motifs but written by sophisticated modern authors', much favoured by the German Romantics.[21] Its development was promoted by Goethe's short narrative simply entitled *Das Märchen* (1795) and filled with enigmatic and esoteric symbolism. Hoffmann probably paid particular attention to the *Märchen* in Novalis's novel *Heinrich von Ofterdingen* (1802), which is told by the magician Klingsohr, starts in Atlantis (a further stimulus for *The Golden Pot*),

Title vignette for 'Nussknacker und Mausekönig' ('The Nutcracker and the Mouse-King'), 1816, showing the two title characters as antagonists; based on a design by Hoffmann.

and essentially tells the triadic Romantic narrative of the fall from primal harmony into discord and conflict and the ultimate restoration of harmony on a higher level. *The Golden Pot* offers another version of this narrative, especially in the myth that is interwoven with events in Dresden.

The two *Märchen* Hoffmann wrote specifically for children are distinctly frightening. 'Nussknacker und Mausekönig' ('The Nutcracker and the Mouse-King'), generally known in English as *The Nutcracker*, especially since it inspired Tchaikovsky's 1892 ballet of the same name, and 'Das fremde Kind' ('The Strange Child') were written for the children of Hoffmann's friend Hitzig, published in two volumes of Christmas stories and collected in *The Serapion Brethren*. Both tales are told by the narrator Lothar and criticized by his friends, who claim that the stories' many subtleties will be lost on children and that the introduction of fairy-tale elements into the everyday world creates an ironic tone fatal to the simplicity and naivety of a children's story. Lothar protests that one should not underestimate children: lively, imaginative children reject the insipid stuff often dished up as *Märchen*, and 'it is astonishing how accurately and vividly their minds apprehend a great deal that is wholly lost on many a clever-clever papa' (H IV, 306). He does not, however, rebut the charge that irony in children's stories is directed more at adults than at children.

Another possible criticism is that these stories are too frightening. In 'The Nutcracker', Marie lies awake fearing an attack by the seven-headed Mouse King, who crawls into her bed and blackmails her into handing over all her sweets to save the Nutcracker's life. She cuts her arm on the glass-fronted cupboard in her bedroom and might have been severely injured; the incident has disturbing sexual overtones. Hoffmann's story conveys a truth which at that time was not yet admitted in literature: that children have an imaginative life, often full of anxieties, which they feel adults would not understand. It also offers the possibility of overcoming childhood terrors.[22] This tale, still widely popular as a Christmas story, helped to found a tradition of children's literature involving real menace. The novel *The Princess and the Goblin* (1872) by George MacDonald, an author himself steeped in German Romantic literature, is a crucial landmark.

In 'The Strange Child', the two children, Christlieb and Felix, are tormented by a harsh tutor, Magister Tinte (Master Ink), who is hostile to the imagination and turns out to be a huge bluebottle in disguise. A strange child who visits them cannot save them from misfortune. Their father dies, perhaps cursed by Magister Tinte, and they and their mother are driven from their home and reduced to beggary. But the strange child finally reappears to them, urges them not to forget him and prophesies that they will be happy, and so it turns out: they are taken in by kindly relatives, and all their future undertakings are successful. The message is that one must not lose contact with the imagination one possessed in one's childhood. It reads like a secularized version of Jesus' assurance to his disciples that he would send the Holy Spirit, the Comforter, to sustain them in his absence (John 14:16–17). Here, as in many other ways, Romantic literature transposes a religious statement into the language of art.

Two particularly elaborate stories are *Märchen* that in different ways follow the model of *The Golden Pot*. *Klein Zaches genannt Zinnober* (Little Zaches, aka Cinnabar, written in 1818) is set in an imaginary petty principality from which the Enlightenment has banished most of the fairies. One of the few survivors, Rosabelverde, takes pity on a poor peasant woman with a deformed and dwarfish son.[23] She gives the son, Zaches, a gift whereby everything good achieved by anybody else in his presence will be attributed to him. This enables Zaches to shine in society. When the student Balthasar (a colourless version of Anselmus) recites a poem, everyone showers praise on Zaches for his divine poetic gift. Under the name Cinnabar he is made a minister of state, receives the Order of the Green-Spotted Tiger, and pays court to Balthasar's love interest, the charming Candida, daughter of Professor Mosch Terpin. With the aid of the magician Prosper Alpanus (a Lindhorst-like figure), Balthasar discovers that Cinnabar's magic power resides in three red hairs that the fairy planted on his head. He tears them out; everyone perceives Zaches in his true shape, and the little creature, in a panic, jumps into a 'beautiful silver vessel with handles' (that is, a chamber-pot; H III, 637) and is drowned. There is a symmetry here, for in Hoffmann's original conception of *The Golden Pot* Anselmus was to use a chamber-pot and be transformed into a monkey (H II/1, 747). This story was a favourite of Karl Marx, perhaps because in Zaches, who magically misappropriates others' achievements, he perceived 'as apt a symbol of alienation as may be found in world literature'.[24]

Little Zaches shares with another late *Märchen*, *Master Flea*, a satirical take on how narrow-minded materialist views of nature ignore its beauty and mystery. In *Little Zaches*, Professor Mosch Terpin, author of a little compendium containing a complete account of nature, has founded his reputation on the discovery that darkness results from the absence of light. His antagonist, Balthasar, complains that his experiments are 'deliberate mockery of the divine being whose breath we feel in nature' (H III, 555; this recalls Anselmus's insight into the language of nature at the end of the First Vigil). Prosper Alpanus, however, recognizes in Balthasar 'a pure heart' in which 'those chords still echo that belong to the distant land of divine marvels which is my home' (H III, 618). In *Master Flea* we meet two scientists, identified as the microscopist Antonie van Leeuwenhoek and the entomologist Jan Swammerdam, who are inexplicably still alive in modern Frankfurt and who are castigated for the irreverence with which they pry into the wonders of nature. This anti-science polemic need not impress us: the example of Goethe is enough to prove that investigation of the natural world is compatible with appreciation and reverence for nature.

The scientists play a crucial part in the narrative, however, because they are anxious to recapture the title character, the ruler of all the fleas. The hero, Peregrinus Tyss, has inadvertently saved Master Flea from his enemies, and is rewarded with good advice and a magic glass, which, when inserted in his eye, enables Peregrinus to perceive people's thoughts. Peregrinus himself is a childlike figure, but in a different way from Anselmus. Having left Frankfurt for three years as a young man, only to return to find his parents dead, he lives in seclusion, with only his old nurse Aline for company. The opening chapter tells how on Christmas Eve he goes shopping and buys a large number of toys, laying them out as presents for himself. This scene, making the reader do a double take with the revelation that Peregrinus is not a child but a man of 36, is as disturbing as anything Hoffmann ever wrote, for it portrays a man desperately trying to recreate the secure world of his childhood and ignore the trauma of its destruction.

The accidental intervention of Master Flea catapults Peregrinus into the adult world. He gives his presents to a poor family with many children. On his visit to the family, they are joined by a beautiful and charming lady who seems to know Peregrinus, though he has no idea who she is, and who insists on coming home with him. To Peregrinus's further astonishment, she begs him to release the 'prisoner' who is locked up in his house. Eventually it appears that this prisoner is none other than Master Flea, who was hiding in a box in the toyshop where Peregrinus went shopping. The lady, apparently a Dutchwoman named Dörtje Elwerdink, wants to possess the flea for pressing reasons of her own. As the story continues, it emerges that the main characters have dual identities: Dörtje is a tulip (an allusion to the Dutch craze for tulips) and Peregrinus's surly friend George Pepusch is a thistle; both come from the magical lands of Famagusta and Samarkand (nothing to do with the real places bearing these names), ruled by King Sekakis, who corresponds to Peregrinus.[25]

Master Flea ends with Peregrinus turning his back on the magical world and committing himself to the real world of modern Frankfurt. He marries Röschen, the daughter of the poor artisan to whose children he gave presents. He resolves to make no more use of Master Flea's magic eyeglass, because when he tried it out he found that other people's thoughts were mostly malicious. Master Flea remains the guardian spirit of his house. Dörtje and her lover George Pepusch, however, commit themselves to their botanical identities. Their mutual yearning, symbolized by the *Cactus grandiflorus*, which flowers magnificently once every hundred years, ends in a rapturous and ultra-Romantic *Liebestod*, whereas

Peregrinus and Röschen choose reasonable happiness without such passionate intensity.

There is much more in *Master Flea*, including a legal theme discussed in the next chapter. Hoffmann, who completed the story shortly before his death, seems not to have been in entire control of his material. As Dörtje professes to need a flea bite to prevent her from shrivelling up into an old woman, there are hints that she is somehow identical with Aline, Peregrinus's aged nurse. Aline is associated with Henri-Montan Berton's opera *Aline, Queen of Golconda*, which Hoffmann had conducted in 1808 in Bamberg. Golconda is both an actual place in India and a metaphor for untold wealth. During Peregrinus's three years away from Frankfurt he spent time with Pepusch in India. But Hoffmann never got round to developing these tantalizing hints into a distinct narrative strand.

Other Media, Other Texts

Music and painting often feature in Hoffmann's stories, giving them an intermedial character. Some stories, too, are closely related to other texts, either by contemporary Romantic writers or by Shakespeare.

A light and amusing tale, 'Die Fermate' (The Fermata, 1819), appears early in *The Serapion Brethren* and serves to lighten the mood after the story of Krespel. Its title denotes a pause in which a singer delivers an artificially lengthened note or trill. The story starts by describing a painting by Johann Erdmann Hummel (1769–1852) that Hoffmann saw exhibited at the Berlin Academy. Two Italian women are sitting in an Italian bower, one singing, the other playing the guitar, both directed by a black-clad *abbate* (a secular cleric); the singer is supposed to be uttering a *fermata*. Theodor, the narrator, relates the painting to his own experience. As a boy, he was (like Hoffmann) receiving rather pedestrian music lessons from his uncle, who did not approve of singing. The uncle was nevertheless persuaded to arrange a concert for two visiting Italian sisters, Lauretta and Teresina. Theodor was so entranced by the art of song that he travelled around Germany with the women, composing songs for them and accompanying them on the piano. At one concert, however, Lauretta stretched out a *fermata* to such intolerable length that Theodor stopped it by striking a chord on the piano. Lauretta was eventually appeased, but Theodor broke with the pair when he overheard them mocking him. Fourteen years later Theodor again meets them in Rome, in the bower exactly like the one painted by Hummel; Lauretta is in a fury because her overextended trill has again been spoiled, this time by the *abbate* who appears in the painting. Theodor helps to calm her down, and the four spend a pleasant evening together, but in his eyes the sisters have lost the charm that enchanted him as a boy, especially as they still dress in the same, now inappropriately youthful fashion. The story combines several art forms in a mildly melancholy reflection on the disillusionment that comes with the passage of time.

Another painting, this time by Carl Wilhelm Kolbe the Younger (1781–1853), prompts the story 'Doge und Dogaresse' (The Doge and His Wife, 1819), but this time the discussion of the painting is more closely integrated with the narrative. The painting, displayed in Berlin in 1816, shows the elderly Venetian doge Marino Faliero (1274–1355), his much younger wife Annunziata, and a young man, Antonio, who was formerly in love with her. The ships visible in the background are preparing to celebrate the doge's symbolic marriage with the sea. In the painting's frame is inscribed a short poem, intimating that the doge's wife does not love her husband. As Hoffmann knew from his research, Marino plotted to seize absolute power in Venice, but was detected and executed. In Hoffmann's story, after Marino's execution Antonio and Annunziata try to flee by boat, but they are drowned, and their *Liebestod* – claimed as among the first in literature – is attributed to the revenge of the sea, 'the jealous widow of the beheaded Falieri [*sic*]' (*Tales* 308).[26] After the Brethren hear this story, told by Ottmar, they look afresh at the painting and perceive greater depths in it: the doge's vanity, his wife's melancholy and the gathering clouds that now seem to proceed from 'a hostile power' threatening 'death and destruction' (*Tales* 309).[27]

Literary intertexts helped to inspire several of the stories. Knowledge of these intertexts can give a more precise understanding of Hoffmann's aims and achievements. We have already seen that Cardillac in 'Mademoiselle de Scudery', in his ambivalence, is a version of Kleist's Michael Kohlhaas. In 'Die Bergwerke zu Falun' ('The Mines at Falun', 1819), Hoffmann drew on several sources. One is G. H. Schubert, who reports in his *Ansichten* how a young miner in the great copper mines at Falun in central Sweden was buried in a rockfall; fifty years later the man's corpse was found perfectly preserved in vitriolic water and was recognized by his former lover, now aged and frail.[28] Hoffmann elaborates this well-attested story by giving names to the characters – the miner is Elis Fröbom, his lover is Ulla, daughter of Persohn Dahlsjö – and providing much detail about mineralogy and Swedish customs and topography, taken from travel books.[29] He includes an evocative and scientifically exact description of the enormous pit, comparing it to Dante's Hell (*Tales* 321). Literary stimulus came from the symbol-laden descriptions of mines in Novalis's *Heinrich von Ofterdingen* and Tieck's *Der Runenberg* (The Runic Mountain, 1804). Tieck's hero is torn between married life on the plain and the allure of the mine, where he is attracted by a mysterious figure, the Mountain Queen. Hoffmann's Elis is likewise torn between Ulla and the Mountain Queen, who is said to inhabit the depths of the mine, though,

The Great Pit at the Falun mine.

in contrast to Tieck's story, she appears only in dreams.[30] This makes Hoffmann's story less of a supernatural tale and more of a psychological study in obsession. Elis's fascination with the hidden world of minerals makes him, on the morning of his and Ulla's wedding, pay a final visit to the mine, from which he never returns. The other world, which in *The Golden Pot* represents Anselmus's salvation, here fatally lures Elis away from possible happiness in the human world.

Novalis's novel is also an intertext for the story 'Der Kampf der Sänger' ('The Singers' Contest', 1818) though in detail Hoffmann's story closely follows the *Nuremberg Chronicle* (1697) by the historian Johann Christoph Wagenseil, which includes an account of medieval singing competitions. At a singing contest in the famous Wartburg fortress, the victor, who wins the hand of Countess Mathilde, is Wolfframb von Eschinbach (the thirteenth-century poet generally known as Wolfram von Eschenbach). A contrast with him and the other poets is provided by Heinrich von Ofterdingen, an unhappy, conflicted character who is tormented by unrequited love for Mathilde. He is advised to seek help from the magician Klingsohr, who summons up a demon called Nasias. Instead of Heinrich, who absents himself, the conflict with the demon is fought out by Wolfframb, who as a devout and spiritually healthy Christian poet manages to vanquish the demon. A letter from Heinrich announces that in the meantime he has been cured of his melancholy, and we are told that he goes on to have a successful poetic career. He is related to Novalis's Ofterdingen as a negative to a positive. Novalis's exemplary poet, sent by a richly symbolic dream on the arch-Romantic quest for the blue flower, seems destined to win the love of Mathilde, who in his version is the daughter of the admirable poet Klingsohr. Hoffmann's Ofterdingen represents the familiar Romantic figure of the unhappy, tortured artist, often embodied in Hoffmann's works by Johannes Kreisler. It disturbs the unity of the story that the focus shifts from Heinrich to Wolfframb, who defeats the demon that would probably have destroyed Heinrich, and that we do not see how Heinrich is cured; he himself attributes his cure to the successful outcome of Wolfframb's conflict with Nasias. The underlying problem is that Hoffmann recreates the medieval setting in what were already conventional terms, in which the tormented modern poet is either an incongruous or a merely negative figure.[31] Hoffmann's Middle Ages cannot accommodate a Kreisler.

If Hoffmann had a favourite writer, it was probably Shakespeare. Innumerable quotations from Shakespeare are worked into his texts. The novella 'Die Brautwahl' ('The Choosing of the Bride', 1820) explicitly borrows motifs from *The Merchant of Venice*. The potential bride of the title, Albertine Vosswinckel, daughter of a high-ranking Berlin civil servant, has three suitors: a pedantic but good-natured bureaucrat, Tusmann (recalling Heerbrand in *The Golden Pot*); a foolish young fop, Baron Benjamin Dümmerl (from *dumm*, stupid); and the young painter Edmund Lehsen. The last has the support of the goldsmith Leonhard Turnhäuser, who, like the painter in *The Devil's Elixirs*, is a revenant from an earlier century and has some supernatural powers. The goldsmith persuades Albertine's father to adopt from *The Merchant of Venice* the method of inviting each suitor to choose from three caskets. The successful suitor will be the one who chooses the casket containing Albertine's portrait.

This entertaining story is rendered less palatable by its antisemitic element. Baron Dümmerl, accompanied by his uncle Manasseh, a Jew in traditional garb, is a young Jew with the affected manners that were often thought characteristic of emancipated Jews trying too hard to assimilate to Western society. On the one hand, the Berlin circles in which Hoffmann moved were hospitable to Jewish people, especially but not only those who had converted to Christianity. Jewish hostesses such as Rahel Varnhagen entertained a variety of guests at their salons. Hoffmann's close friend Hitzig, born Isaac Elias Itzig, had been baptized in 1799 as Julius Eduar, but in 1809 added an H to his surname to make it sound less Jewish.[32] On the other hand, antisemitic pamphlets were in circulation; the reactionary Christlich-deutsche Tischgesellschaft (Christian German Dining Club), to which Hoffmann's acquaintance Clemens Brentano belonged, listened approvingly to violently antisemitic speeches; the cruel comedy about would-be assimilated Jews *Unser Verkehr* (The Company We Keep) by Karl Sessa played to packed

Unknown artist, *E.T.A. Hoffmann*, before 1822, oil on wood.

houses across Germany in 1815; and in 1819 anti-Jewish riots, with no deaths but much violence and looting, took place in Hamburg, Frankfurt and other German towns.[33] Hoffmann's friend Devrient played not only, as is mentioned in 'The Choosing of the Bride' (*Tales* 400), Shylock in *The Merchant of Venice*, but the leading role in *The Company We Keep* as a pretentious young Jew (resembling Dümmerl); he used to perform scenes from it to amuse Hoffmann and his fellow drinkers. A visitor, Adam Oehlenschläger, heard Hoffmann tell a funny story about a Jew who claimed to be haunted by his dead wife as part of an elaborate scam (A 417).

One might accuse Hoffmann of appealing to popular prejudice in his depiction not only of Jews but of women. Albertine Vosswinckel is represented as a charming but shallow young lady with all the requisite fashionable accomplishments. After winning her in the contest of the caskets, Edmund goes to Rome for a year to practise painting. During that time he and Albertine exchange fewer and fewer letters, and the end of the story suggests that she will probably abandon Edmund and marry instead a handsome young trainee lawyer. Similarly, the strong-willed Veronika in *The Golden Pot*, who resorts even to magic to capture Anselmus, is happy finally to settle for *Hofrat* Heerbrand. In another *Serapion Brethren* tale, 'Der Artushof' (The Artushof, the name of a building in Danzig/ Gdańsk) (*Tales*, 133), the charms of a woman named Christina are described with an irony that makes one even more suspicious of the narrator's praise of Clara in 'The Sandman'. At the end Christina marries her father's bookkeeper, while the hero, the painter Traugott, after wasting a year in pursuit of an inaccessible woman, is happy to settle for an attractive young lady in Rome who returns his advances, which would seem to overcome the conflict between love and art that proves fatal for so many figures in Hoffmann's fiction.[34]

To call Hoffmann's portrayal of women misogynistic may be too severe, but it is hard to find in his works a female figure who by present-day standards is not disparaged, however mildly, or idealized like Aurelie in *The Devil's Elixirs*. As we shall see in the next chapter, however, the female characters in the novel *The Life and Opinions of the Tomcat Murr* – Julia Benzon, her mother and, in particular, Princess Hedwiga – move from stereotypes to being intriguing and problematic characters in their own right.

4

Hoffmann in Berlin, 1814–22

Hoffmann stayed in Berlin until his death in 1822, living at a pace that must have shortened his life. His opera *Undine* was performed; he wrote reflections on opera as an art combining words and music; he satisfied publishers' demands for fiction, some of it collected in *The Serapion Brethren*, the rest scattered in periodicals; and he produced two of his masterpieces, the story *Prinzessin Brambilla* (Princess Brambilla, 1821), which is closely related to his enthusiasm for opera, and the novel *The Life and Opinions of the Tomcat Murr*, which was left unfinished on his death. His day job, as a senior judge, became ever more demanding and even politically perilous. And he led a convivial social life, though the sheer amount of writing he produced compels us to discard as a myth the idea that he spent every evening drinking with friends in Lutter & Wegner's wine cellar.

Opera

Hoffmann set out his aesthetics of opera in the fictional dialogue 'The Poet and the Composer', which, following its original publication in 1813, was reprinted in the first volume of *The Serapion Brethren* in 1819. In the framing conversation among the Brethren that precedes the latter version, the main theme that is formulated is the relation between words and music in opera, and how closely the two should be combined. Lothar maintains that 'music and word flow from the inspired poet and composer at the *same* instant' (C 189).

Of the two partners in the dialogue, Ferdinand, a soldier fresh from the military campaign of 1813, maintains that words and music

Wilhelm Hensel, *E.T.A. Hoffmann*, 1821, pencil drawing.

must be separate, whereas Ludwig, a poet who has done his best to avoid even noticing the conflict, advocates their unity. He condemns the customary practice whereby music and libretto are so distinct that they barely fit together:

> Most so-called operas are merely inane plays with singing added, and the total lack of dramatic force, imputed now to the libretto, now to the music, is entirely attributable to the dead weight of

> successive scenes with no inner poetic relationship or poetic truth that might kindle the music into life. (C 200)

He acknowledges that Mozart and Gluck are exceptions. True composers like Mozart know how to choose texts that are worthy of their talents, while 'the magnificent Gluck, who stands forth like a demigod' (C 201), composed operas of tragic depth.[1] In the past, great tragic operas were composed in a style akin to that of church music, which helps to explain their profundity:

> In the majority of older tragic operas, such as are sadly no longer written and set to music, it is again the true heroism of action and the inner strength of character and situation which so powerfully seize the spectator. The dark, mysterious forces governing gods and men pass visibly before his eyes, and he listens as the eternal, immutable decrees of providence to which even the gods are subject are proclaimed in strange and ominous tones. (C 200–201)

Not only do most present-day operas fail to reach such standards, but their triviality is reinforced by the practice of alternating music with spoken dialogue, so that no serious or truly moving narrative has time to develop.

These strictures express Hoffmann's own ambitions. While still in Bamberg he had read Fouqué's tale *Undine*, in which he immediately saw material for an opera. In a vaguely medieval setting, the knight Huldbrand falls in love with Undine, who is the adoptive child of poor fisherfolk but in reality an elemental spirit. Her parents, against the will of her uncle Kühleborn, sent her into the human world so that she might win the love of a man and thus acquire a soul, instead of being dissolved into the elements on her death. Huldbrand, however, deserts her for Bertalda, who turns out to be the long-lost child of the fisherfolk but shows no affection for her real parents. On the day of her wedding to Huldbrand, Bertalda demands that a bricked-up well be opened; Undine, who has been imprisoned in the well, emerges and kisses Huldbrand to death.[2]

Arthur Rackham, 'Soon she was lost to sight in the Danube', illustration from Friedrich de la Motte Fouqué's *Undine*, adapted by W. L. Courtney (1909).

Hoffmann wrote to the author: 'I cannot put into words how deeply moved I was by the profound nature of the romantic characters in the story' (15 August 1812). However, as Hoffmann was not sure that he could write dramatic poetry, he asked Fouqué, through the intermediacy of Hitzig, to adapt his story into a libretto, and to his delight Fouqué promptly agreed. The text, which Fouqué delivered in November 1812, changes the ending: instead of pursuing Huldbrand to give him the fatal kiss, Undine draws him down into the well to his death, like the water-nixie in Goethe's poem 'Der Fischer' ('The Fisherman', 1779).[3]

Hoffmann finished composing the music in August 1814, and the opera had its premiere on 3 August 1816. Playing to a full house, it was a stunning success, thanks in part to the stage sets designed by the painter and architect Karl Friedrich Schinkel (1781–1841), who had recently designed the sets for a memorable production of *The Magic Flute*, but also to the leading lady Johanna Eunike (1798–1856), who had already sung Pamina in *The Magic Flute* and Zerlina in *Don Giovanni*, and whom Fouqué praised as 'exceptionally charming and skilful' (A 337). The composer Carl Maria von Weber (1786–1826), who knew Hoffmann personally, reviewed it enthusiastically for the *AMZ*. His praise implied that the opera met the standards set by Hoffmann in 'The Poet and the Composer'. It was one of the most ingenious and intelligent (*geistvollsten*) works of the modern age, sustained by the development of profound ideas (*tief überlegten Ideengang*). In contrast to the operas that Hoffmann criticized for alternating jerkily between song and speech, its movement had unbroken unity and continuity:

> The music is in a single mould, and after repeated hearings the present writer cannot remember a single passage that even for a moment broke the magic spell cast by the composer . . . [Hoffmann] goes steadily forward, visibly guided by the determination to achieve dramatic truth and intensity instead of holding up the swift progress of the drama or shackling it in any way. (quoted C 177)

Having seen many years ago an excellent production by students at Oxford, I can testify also to the opera's dramatic qualities. In particular, the sinister figure of Kühleborn (appearing, in the performance I saw, in a robe that is suitably dripping wet) towers over the action as he plots to lure Undine back to her watery domain and take revenge on Huldbrand. The evocation of nature, a force both seductive and sinister, has been well described by the music historian John Warrack:

> Hoffmann wrote music strong enough to give the waters and the forests their own power, an element alongside the characters and working upon them. The storm breaking into the overture, with Huldbrand and the Fisherman calling into the darkness after Undine; the scene in which the waters and their spirits show their menace to [the Christian priest] Heilmann; the Act II finale as mist rises to envelop Undine, cursed by Huldbrand, and return her to her element; Undine's final appearance out of the opened well to surround Huldbrand with the deadly embrace of water: these scenes and others bring Nature into musical drama in far more than token form.[4]

It has also been noted that Hoffmann uses 'recurring themes to identify characters or situations', a technique that would be developed by Weber and on a massive scale by Wagner.[5] Wagner, moreover, achieved an aspiration that always eluded Hoffmann: to be both composer and poet.

Undine went through fourteen performances by July 1817. On 17 July, however, the theatre burned down, and Schinkel's stage sets and the costumes were destroyed. As the Hoffmanns lived next to the theatre, their lives were in danger, but they kept their heads and moved furniture and curtains into a safer back room (to Hippel, 15 December 1817). The fire, however, ended *Undine*'s run, and it was soon overshadowed by Weber's hugely popular *The Freeshooter*, first performed in Berlin on 4 May 1821. Hoffmann knew that his professional duties would not leave him time to compose another opera. Even the score of the overture he had composed for Fouqué's one-act play *Thassilo*, performed on 22 October 1815, was lost in the theatre fire.

Undine, however, embodied only one of the possibilities contemplated in 'The Poet and the Composer'. Ludwig speaks passionately on behalf of 'romantic opera', that is, opera that is romantic in a different sense from *Undine*. *Undine* appealed to the Romantics' liking for stories with a supernatural element, usually dating from the Middle Ages. Ludwig welcomes the supernatural in opera, but not as 'a merely whimsical series of pointless magical happenings' (c 196). Rather, the supernatural should intimate to us the existence of a higher spiritual realm, and this requires exceptional poetic inspiration:

> Only the inspired poet of genius can write a truly romantic opera, for only he can bring before our eyes the wonderful apparitions of the spirit-realm; carried on his wings we soar across the abyss that formerly separated us from it, and soon at home in that strange land we accept the miracles that are seen

Caricatural depiction by Hoffmann of the fire at the Schauspielhaus on the Gendarmenmarkt, 29 July 1817, and the resulting danger to Berlin's Seehandlung building caused by C.W.F. Unzelmann's burning wig and the rescue of the state credit by a guardsman.

to take place as natural consequences of the influence of higher natures on our lives. (c 196)

In romantic opera, accordingly, language is 'raised to a higher power' and 'takes the form of song' (c 197). Here, Hoffmann is particularly concerned with the literary aspect of opera, with the libretto. And as his example of a 'truly romantic poet of genius' (c 197), he gives the Venetian poet Count Carlo Gozzi (1720–1806). Gozzi combined the Italian tradition of *commedia dell'arte*, relying on improvised dialogue and stock characters such as Harlequin, Columbine and Pantaloon, with elaborate, serio-comic supernatural events, sometimes drawn from Italian fairy tales. His serious characters speak in verse, while the *commedia dell'arte* figures improvise their lines. He conducted a literary feud with the dramatist Carlo Goldoni (1707–1793), who specialized in recognizably realistic comedies suited to middle-class audiences, and the ex-Jesuit Pietro Chiari (1711–1785), who wrote sentimental comedies and neoclassical tragedies. Hoffmann implicitly condemned these writers as 'moralistic playwrights, grubbing among the trivialities of everyday life' (Goldoni) and would-be heroic tragedians who unintentionally produce comedy (Chiari; both c 200).[6] Gozzi's 'fables' (*fiabe*) satisfy Hoffmann's criteria by combining tragic with comic elements and by intimating the existence of a 'shadowy spirit-realm' from which 'the spirits emerge into the world and enmesh men in the mysterious fate that governs their own movements' (c 199). Having listened to Ludwig's highly circumstantial summary of the plot of Gozzi's *Il corvo* (The Raven, 1761), Ferdinand is won over and declares: 'Only in a truly romantic work can the comic be so smoothly blended with the tragic that they combine into a single overall effect and seize the listener's spirit in a strange and magical way' (c 200).

Gozzi was important for Hoffmann throughout his literary career. In an early letter to Hippel, he invokes 'Saint Gozzi' (26 September 1805). Describing to Kunz, on 19 August 1813, his first idea for *The Golden Pot*, in which Anselmus was to urinate in the pot and be transformed into a monkey, Hoffmann adds:

'You notice, my friend, the shades of Gozzi and Faffner!' Gozzi's characters often undergo fairy-tale transformations. I support the conjecture that 'Faffner' is a mistake (probably an editorial mistranscription) for 'Haffner', and that Hoffmann was referring to the popular Viennese dramatist Philipp Hafner (1735–1764), whose magical comedies were often performed in south German theatres.[7] Serpentina in *The Golden Pot* is a version of the heroine of Gozzi's *La donna serpente* (The Serpent Woman, 1762).[8]

Princess Brambilla

Gozzi is most markedly present in the long *Märchen* set in Rome and entitled *Princess Brambilla*.[9] In the preface, Hoffmann associates Gozzi with another long-standing favourite of his, the painter Jacques Callot, in whose 'manner' he had claimed his *Fantasy-Pieces* were written. For his 44th birthday, on 24 January 1820, his friend David Koreff gave him Callot's *Balli di Sfessania* (1622), a cycle of 24 etchings named after a Neapolitan dance and depicting pairs of fantastic and grotesque figures from the *commedia dell'arte*. Hoffmann chose eight of the cycle and had copies engraved as illustrations to *Brambilla*. He also took from Callot the term *capriccio* for *Brambilla*'s subtitle. A capriccio was originally an improvised piece of music, but Callot applied the term to visual art in the title of his series *Capricci di varie figure* (1617). Hoffmann borrowed it to mean a whimsical series of literary inventions based not on mimetic realism but on the fancy of the writer. He thus not only founded the genre of the literary capriccio but is plausibly claimed to have brought it 'to a point of artistic perfection which is later never equalled'.[10] Having drawn the reader's attention to the illustrations from Callot, Hoffmann quotes Gozzi's view that fantastic inventions are not enough to provide a work with a soul: that must come from an idea, based on a philosophical view of life (H III, 769).

The central character in *Princess Brambilla*, Giglio Fava, is an actor who performs in plays by Gozzi. In Chapter One, he comes straight from the theatre where he has been playing the role of

Jacques Callot, 'Fracischina and Gian Farina', etching from the series *Balli di Sfessania* (Dance of Sfessania), 1617–27.

Prince Taer in Gozzi's *Il mostro turchino* (The Blue Monster). He recounts a dream in which a beautiful princess declared her love for him; this earns him a scolding from his girlfriend Giacinta. Giacinta has just been lamenting her poverty and wishing she were wealthy enough to own the magnificent dress that she is in the process of busily sewing. Both hero and heroine, then, are obsessed by romantic dreams. Soon their vivid imaginations lead them to confuse fantasy with reality. Since the magnificent dress fits Giacinta perfectly, she fancies that she is the lady for whom it is destined. Giglio similarly fails to distinguish his real self from the character he impersonates: earlier that day, we learn, he was 'looking somewhat like Prince Taer and feeling exactly like him' (*GP* 128).[11] He is said to invite the admiration of the audience and to ignore his fellow actors, and to be as vain as a young cockerel. In short, he misuses his imagination. Instead of allowing his real self to be absorbed into his role, he uses his role to nourish his own egotism.

In the course of the story, Giglio and Giacinta are cured of their vanity by having their identities doubled. Their fantasy selves split off and assume independent existences as Princess Brambilla and her lover, the Assyrian prince Cornelio Chiapperi. This process, stage-managed by the apparent mountebank Celionati – a clear counterpart to Lindhorst in *The Golden Pot* – with supernatural aid, also provides Giglio with a lesson in acting. Near the beginning of the story his style of acting is described as pompous and declamatory, with extravagant gestures. His self-regarding vanity has to give way to a loss of self; only by losing himself in his role will he be truly himself and also a true actor. He seems to have made some progress by Chapter Four, when he returns to Giacinta's flat and finds her sewing. She talks mysteriously of her impending marriage to a prince, and Giglio replies that he is about to marry Princess Brambilla. Yet their conversation sounds very like a game, especially when Giacinta says that her husband's kingdom is near Bergamo (the provenance of some *commedia dell'arte* characters), and both agree that their kingdoms had better be transferred to Frascati, a convenient distance from Rome. Even earlier, Giglio's tragic ranting has been accompanied by self-mockery as well as some good-natured jibing from Giacinta. It almost seems that the learning process is already over, and that Giglio and Giacinta are now able to use their fantasies as material for a game, while remaining anchored in reality.

However, Giglio has to undergo still deeper self-estrangement. Like Anselmus, he is tempted and falls. His tempter is the appalling tragic playwright the Abbate Chiari, who persuades him to distrust Celionati. In what Hoffmann ironically calls the 'pleasant low-water period, when the human spirit rejoices in perfect sobriety' (that is, a state of prosaic, unimaginative common sense, perfectly compatible with admiration for the Abbate's wooden tragedies), Giglio relapses into his former vanity, dressing up as a prince and boldly entering the Pistoia Palace in search of Princess Brambilla. Instead of finding her, however, he is caught and put in a cage as a 'feather-brain' (Hoffmann's word, *Gelbschnabel*, means a fledgling bird and also a simpleton), an episode corresponding to Anselmus's imprisonment in the bottle. This does not cure his vanity, however; indeed, Celionati encourages his conviction that he is Prince Cornelio Chiapperi, and that Princess Brambilla has foisted Giacinta upon him so that she herself may pursue the wretched actor Giglio Fava.

That evening sees the encounter between Giglio's two selves, the *commedia* mask as Pantaloon that he assumed earlier, and the mask with silk breeches and pink stockings that he wore in Chapter One. The combatants display affection as well as antagonism – after all, they are the same person – but in the end Giglio is killed and his corpse removed amid the merriment of the populace. Later we are told that Giglio was only made of cardboard, that his health was ruined by overindulgence in Chiari's indigestible tragedies (literary junk food, so to speak) and that in any case his acting was worthless. We learn this from an unnamed young man of mild manners, who describes himself as Prince Cornelio Chiapperi. This of course is Giglio; but not the old, vain, shallow Giglio. He has killed his former self and assumed the identity of the Assyrian prince; but this new and always fragile identity represents the transition to a new version of his self as Giglio Fava.

Once this transition is complete, the story of Giglio and Giacinta converges with the myth of Urdar, which has accompanied their narrative ever since Chapter Three. This likewise falls into two phases, each dealing with estrangement and its overcoming. The tale of King Ophioch and Queen Liris, like the myth in *The Golden Pot*, concerns humanity's estrangement from an original harmony with nature. Reunion is achieved, on a higher plane, when Ophioch and Liris awake from sleep and look into the well of Urdar. There they behold their world turned upside down and thus transformed into 'a magnificent new world full of life and joy' (*GP* 166). They burst into joyful laughter. As the magus Hermod cryptically explains, man can overcome his estrangement from nature by perceiving himself and his surroundings in the mirror of art. And one particular kind of art is referred to: comedy, in which, as in the waters of Urdar, the world is reflected upside down, reversed, topsy-turvy.

The second phase of the myth concerns the deeper estrangement that sets in after the deaths of Ophioch and Liris.

The over-rational inhabitants of Urdar, now dominated by philosophers (an allusion to the Enlightenment), cannot understand the language of Princess Mystilis, who represents poetry. Misled by an impostor, Mystilis is reduced to a china doll and the court ladies are set to making lace in which a gaudy bird is to be caught. Here the legend intersects with the story of Giglio, for he in his princely outfit is the gaudy bird to be entrapped in the net. However, when Giglio's transformation is completed, he and Giacinta attain self-knowledge, as Ophioch and Liris had originally done. Transported to Urdar, they look into the lake and know themselves for the first time. They laugh and embrace, and Mystilis, now a queen, is reborn from the lotus as a kind of giantess, her feet planted in the maternal soil and her head in the sky, representing the triumph of poetry.

The story ends with Giglio and Giacinta enjoying both self-knowledge and domestic happiness. As a corrective to Giglio's former vanity, Giacinta has now been promoted from seamstress to actress, and the two act in such harmony that they can improvise for long periods without Giglio, at least, noticing. They are also more prosperous than before, thanks to Celionati, who is now revealed as Prince Bastianello di Pistoia. The well of Urdar, he explains, corresponds to the theatre: both are mirrors that reflect reality more truly than any mere mimetic representation.

Princess Brambilla illustrates Hoffmann's conception of humour. This conception is not only symbolized by the well of Urdar but formulated explicitly in the conversation between Celionati and the German artists who meet in the Caffè Greco. Their spokesman, Reinhold, asserts that German humour expresses the underlying principle of irony. Its surface extravagances arise from this deep-seated principle, just as ripples in a stream are produced by a concealed rock. He claims that the grotesque features of Italian comedy, on the other hand, are indulged for their own sake, and provide at most an occasional and distorted reflection of the principle of irony. *Princess Brambilla* as a whole may be called a synthesis of both traditions, combining the inventive theatricality of Italian masks with the profundity of German humour.

Elsewhere Hoffmann elaborates his conception of humour. His Serapion Brethren contrast German humour with French wit, which consists either in laboured puns and bon mots or in attempts at mockery, which rapidly become unkind and distasteful. The conversation of a truly humorous German is like an inexhaustible display of fireworks (H IV, 914, 915), as Hoffmann's conversation, when he was in good form, is reported to have been. But humour has a further, metaphysical dimension. Reviewing works composed for the piano by Philipp Jakob Riotte (1776–1856) and others, Hoffmann observed that 'in music, as everywhere else, true humour springs only from deep seriousness, from the active, lively perception of what is higher' (H II/2, 522). This 'higher' reality is the unknown realm for which, as Hoffmann often says, great music arouses our longing.

The Life and Opinions of the Tomcat Murr

The discrepancy between our intuitions and our everyday reality can give rise to humour, but it can also be felt as painful, even tragic. This is the experience of Johannes Kreisler, the composer trapped among philistines who think music a mere social accomplishment and not a portal leading to a higher, ineffable reality. Kreisler's 'musical sufferings' are recounted in the series of short texts collectively entitled *Kreisleriana* that feature in *Fantasy-Pieces*. He is also mentioned by Lindhorst in *The Golden Pot* as a friend of the unnamed narrator (*GP* 81). But he comes into his own in Hoffmann's great novel *The Life and Opinions of the Tomcat Murr*. Only two volumes had been published when Hoffmann died in 1822, leaving tantalizing scope for speculation about how it might have continued.

Murr is an extreme example of the self-conscious novel that disrupts readers' expectations of narrative. Such novels may introduce the narrator as a character in the story (as in the last chapter of *The Golden Pot*), relate events in a sequence widely different from their chronological succession (as in 'The Sandman', where the narrator avoids beginning the story), or in other ways remind readers that the story is fictional. The German Romantics were enthusiastic about such novels, beginning with *Don Quixote* (1605–15), where in Part II the Don and Sancho know that they are characters in Part I and criticize other accounts of their adventures.[12] Romantic readers readily saw Cervantes as a predecessor of Sterne, whose narrator in *The Life and Opinions of Tristram Shandy* (a title Hoffmann adapts for *Murr*) plays with fiction by telling his life story so digressively that well over a hundred pages have passed before the character is born. Both Cervantes and Sterne were among Hoffmann's favourite authors. He also enjoyed the much-read novels of Jean Paul; their author supplied a preface to *Fantasy-Pieces*. Jean Paul's hallmark, however, is a densely allusive style rather than self-conscious narration, and his work, though treasured by devotees, has worn much less well than Hoffmann's more radically innovative fiction.

Murr consists of two narratives, plus a preface in which Hoffmann purports to relate how he took the manuscript to his publisher. One narrative is the autobiography of the cat Murr, who has taught himself to write and fancies himself as a man of letters. The other is the story of the musician Kreisler, Murr's owner. Kreisler's story exists only as a series of fragments, because the cat has torn it up in order to write his autobiography on the back of its sheets. Murr's story is told continuously but is interrupted every so often by a piece of the Kreisler narrative, which usually ends mid-sentence, often at a cliffhanger, after which the editor inserts '*M.f.f.*' (that is, *Murr fährt fort*, rendered in Anthea Bell's translation as '*M. cont.*').

It is part of Hoffmann's irony that the story of the genius Kreisler survives only accidentally and in scraps, whereas that of the complacent philistine Murr is preserved entire. The two narratives also contrast in tone. Murr's story is broad comedy. The cat's literary pretensions, shown by his constant quotations, keep giving him away. He even likes to think he is descended from a famous literary cat, Puss in Boots (*Murr* 49). Kreisler's story, told in the third person, is comparatively serious. It is also full of quotations; many come from Shakespeare – especially his comedies, but plenty also from *Hamlet* – and are adapted to express his situation between an unattainable artistic vision and an uncomprehending public on whom he depends for his daily bread.[13] As a Romantic artist, whose biography in some respects resembles his creator's, Kreisler is a troubled and often frightening character, eccentric in his behaviour and haunted by fear of going mad.[14] His strange antics, as he explains, express his sense of imprisonment within the circles ('Kreisler' comes from *Kreis*, circle) drawn by a 'dark, inscrutable power' (*Murr* 50), and the yearning to escape gives rise to 'humour'. His eccentricity is the defence mounted by a sensitive soul against a hostile world. Late in the novel he finds some peace by retreating to a monastery, where the monks are concerned for his well-being.

The Murr and Kreisler stories do not coincide in time. Here Hoffmann is even bolder in disrupting narrative coherence. In the first part of the Kreisler story that readers are given, his friend and former tutor, the conjuror and court factotum Master Abraham, introduces Kreisler to Murr and tells how he rescued Murr as a kitten from drowning. Chronologically, therefore, this is the beginning of Murr's story, but it comes after the end of Kreisler's experiences. For Master Abraham found Murr when returning home from a festivity at the petty princely court of Sieghartsweiler, where both he and Kreisler have been employed. The festivity, arranged by Master Abraham to celebrate the name day of the princess, was a complete, farcical disaster. As Kreisler was absent (presumably at the monastery), Master Abraham tells him (and the reader) about it.

Sieghartsweiler, populated largely by aristocratic philistines, is almost as uncongenial to Kreisler as the music lessons he was obliged to give to untalented bourgeois (see *Kreisleriana*). His work as *Kapellmeister*, however, is appreciated by at least two people: Julia, the daughter of a court lady known as the *Rätin* (councillor's widow) Benzon, and the Princess Hedwiga. When Kreisler first arrives at Sieghartsweiler, he approaches unannounced through the park. The two girls, unaware of his appointment, are astonished to come across him there, alone, playing the guitar and singing;

Front cover illustration for the first edition of *Lebens-Ansichten des Katers Murr* (1819), engraving by Christian Friedrich Schiele based on a drawing by Hoffmann, showing the tomcat Murr at his writing desk.

Back cover illustration for the first edition of *Lebens-Ansichten des Katers Murr* (1819), engraving by Christian Friedrich Schiele based on a drawing by Hoffmann, showing Kreisler as magician.

he eventually makes an angry speech to the guitar, flings it down and stalks off. Julia is intrigued, but Hedwiga is terrified.

These different reactions anticipate the relationships with Kreisler that the pair develop. Julia, a good, kindly and musically talented young woman – another avatar of Julia Marc – comes to love Kreisler and understand his strange humour as coming 'from the truest, finest of minds' (*Murr* 148). She communicates with Kreisler most intimately through music. They perform an Italian duet (one composed by Hoffmann), sung by Julia to Kreisler's piano accompaniment.[15] It is evoked in lyrical language that conveys sublimated erotic passion:

> But soon both voices rose on the waves of the song like shimmering swans, now aspiring to rise aloft to the radiant, golden clouds with the beat of rushing wings, now to sink dying in a sweet amorous embrace in the roaring current of chords, until deep sighs heralded the proximity of death, and with a wild cry of pain the last *Addio* welled like a fount of blood from the wounded breast (*Murr* 103).

Hedwiga's initial revulsion for Kreisler is also soon transformed into an attraction, which grows when she takes music lessons from him. She is one of Hoffmann's most intriguing characters, and probably the most skilfully drawn and least clichéd of all his female figures. Proud, sensitive and mercurial, she responds intensely to the dangerous, pathological streak in Kreisler's personality. She alarms her affectionate friend Julia by declaring: 'You don't yet know how destructive the pain of life can be. Nature is cruel, she cares only for her healthy children and abandons the sick, she even turns deadly weapons on them' (*Murr* 150). It emerges that Hedwiga is a deeply damaged person. She confides in Kreisler how, as a four-year-old child, neglected by her parents, she was very fond of the court painter Leonhard Ettlinger, who suddenly disappeared. Looking for him in the palace, she found him transformed into a terrifying lunatic who threatened to cut her throat. Hence, along with a passionate nature, the adult Hedwiga has a traumatic fear of sex.

That may explain why she is so taken by Kreisler's evocation of 'the artist's love', in which 'in pure heavenly fire that gives only light and warmth, and does not destroy with fierce flames, there blazes up all the delight, all the ineffable joy of the higher life springing from deep within' (*Murr* 118). Not perceiving Kreisler's irony, Hedwiga is enchanted by this description of a sexless, sublimated love.

Kreisler, Julia and Hedwiga are entangled in a mysterious intrigue that would presumably have been clarified if Hoffmann had completed the novel – though one cannot quite imagine the story ending with a neat explanation in the manner of Hercule Poirot. We know that Prince Irenaeus, the ruler of Sieghartsweiler, and the *Rätin* Benzon had an illicit love affair that produced an illegitimate daughter, now dead. We learn that there is a plot to marry Julia to Prince Ignaz, the sadistic and mentally deficient heir to Sieghartsweiler, and to marry Hedwiga to Prince Hektor, a sinister military officer from Naples. We hear about Master Abraham's liaison with Chiara, a girl with psychic gifts who mysteriously vanished, and we witness how a veiled woman accosts Hedwiga one night and addresses her as 'my poor child' (*Murr* 151). Much as one would like to know the story, however, speculation is as futile as it is tempting.[16]

The story of Kreisler, Julia and Hedwiga is so engaging that some commentators have dismissed the Murr story as a mere comic parody of the *Bildungsroman*. Although this term was seldom used in Hoffmann's day, the concept of the quasi-biographical 'novel of development', supremely exemplified by Goethe's *Wilhelm Meisters Lehrjahre* (Wilhelm Meister's Apprenticeship, 1795–6), was familiar. Murr's narrative is divided into chapters with headings such as 'My Apprentice Months' and 'My Months of Greater Maturity'. Another target for affectionate parody was the autobiographical genre; Hoffmann claimed in 1804 that he had read an outstanding example, Rousseau's *Confessions*, at least thirty times (diary, H I, 347).

It would be unjust, however, to dismiss Murr as a merely ridiculous, let alone contemptible character, or to excise his story and let Kreisler's narrative stand on its own, as the Hoffmann scholar Hans von Müller did in 1903.[17] For if Kreisler resembles

Hoffmann, Murr resembles Hoffmann's real cat, who was also called Murr and whom Hoffmann describes in a letter of 1820 to Friedrich Speyer:

> I recommend to you the exceedingly wise and profound tomcat Murr, who at this moment is lying beside me on a little padded chair and seems absorbed in extraordinary thoughts and fantasies, for he is purring like anything! – A *real tomcat* of great beauty (he is portrayed to the life on the cover of the book) and even greater intelligence, whom I brought up, inspired the bizarre joke that is woven into the really very serious book.
> (1 May 1820, H VI, 178)

In November 1821 Murr died, to the great grief of Hoffmann and Mischa. Hoffmann sent his friends a black-bordered death notice, running:

> During the night between the 29th and 30th of November this year, my dear, much loved disciple Kater Murr passed away in the fourth year of his promising life, to awaken to a better existence. Whoever knew the departed youth, whoever saw him walking along the path of virtue and rectitude, will measure my grief and – honour it by silence.
> Hoffmann
> Berlin, 1 December 1821[18]

If the fictional Murr needs defending, one can point out that alongside his literary pretensions he has practical good sense, especially regarding his creature comforts. Reunited with his long-lost mother Mina, he resolves to bring her a herring's head left over from his dinner, but with the Shakespearean reflection 'O Appetite, thy name is Cat!' he devours it himself (*Murr* 36).[19] Despite his literary ambitions, he has his paws firmly on the ground, whereas Kreisler is in danger of being driven mad by his restless creative imagination.[20] Further, the contrast between down-to-earth common sense and lofty but dangerous and perhaps deluded ideals is epitomized by that between Sancho Panza and his master Don Quixote. It would seem that Cervantes's novel has helped to shape Hoffmann's tale on a level more fundamental than that of metafictional play.

Hoffmann the Lawyer

While writing *Murr* and a large body of shorter fiction, Hoffmann was also working as a judge at the Berlin Supreme Court. He dealt especially with difficult cases involving murder or *lèse-majesté*. His judgements are a surprisingly engrossing body of work, fluently written (despite some extraordinarily complex sentences) and displaying his shrewdness, his humanity and his deft command of the law. Some have the fascination of true crime narratives (which is in effect what they are), reminding us that psychological case histories had been a popular fictional form since the late Enlightenment.[21]

Hoffmann's judgements, however, differ sharply from his fiction. While his stories explore the abysses of the self, his judgements cleave to the Kantian principle of 'the moral freedom of humanity' (H VI, 715). He is very reluctant to concede diminished responsibility as an argument for exonerating criminal deeds. Thus in the case of 'Wilhelm S.', who tried unsuccessfully to poison his wife by putting copper oxide in her coffee, Hoffmann easily demolished the defendant's story: the husband claimed that at the crucial moment he did not know what he was doing because he had just drunk four glasses of rum; Hoffmann cited evidence revealing that just before and after the deed Wilhelm S. had played billiards with undiminished concentration. The accused was sentenced to twelve years' imprisonment.

In another case of murder, that of Daniel Schmolling, responsibility was again the key issue. Schmolling had stabbed his lover. His defence claimed that he was subject to a kind of temporary insanity known as *amentia occulta*, which revealed no outward signs of madness, and that he had felt under an unwelcome but irresistible compulsion to kill. Hoffmann reviewed in detail

Ludwig Buchhorn, *E.T.A. Hoffmann*, n.d., pencil drawing created according to E.T.A. Hoffmann's lost chalk drawing, 1823.

the clinical literature, which he had first read in Kunz's library at Bamberg, and found that *amentia occulta* was a mere hypothesis without evidence. It was clear that Schmolling had planned his murder carefully. Only the motive was obscure. But, in Hoffmann's firm view, the law could not plumb the depths of the soul. Anyway, some motivations could be surmised from external circumstances: Schmolling knew that his lover was pregnant and that, having previously lived off her earnings, he would henceforth have to support her and her child.

Hoffmann's refusal to undertake psychological investigation may seem surprising, since in *The Devil's Elixirs* he had entered so intimately into the mind of a fictitious murderer. But for him, as his biographer Rüdiger Safranski has argued in a searching analysis of the Schmolling judgement, fiction was one thing, but a legal case, with its possible momentous consequences, was quite another. The Kantian concept of autonomy preserved human freedom; if doctors had too much licence to declare people incapable of autonomy and to probe the recesses of the psyche, they might gain a dangerous amount of power, like the power-hungry hypnotist Alban in 'The Magnetizer'.[22]

Hoffmann's judgements also show him ready to challenge the authorities. Another case, the Asmann case, concerned someone accused of treason – in 1806 the man had prevented some Prussian soldiers from escaping French captivity and had uttered insulting words about the king. But these soldiers were marauders who terrorized civilians, and the resistance they planned to offer to the French would have resulted in the destruction of an entire village. Hoffmann was able to vindicate Asmann by showing that the soldiers' testimony against him was dubious, self-contradictory and in some cases motivated by revenge.

Another political case was that of Helmina von Chézy (1783–1856), a poet and playwright well known in Berlin literary circles, who in 1815 volunteered to nurse wounded Prussian soldiers in a military hospital. She wrote a letter to the Prussian general Gneisenau complaining of the neglect suffered by the patients. This letter was interpreted as a deliberate insult to the commission appointed to look after wounded soldiers. Chézy was sentenced in her absence to a year's imprisonment and a heavy fine. She appealed to the Prussian minister of justice, Friedrich Leopold von Kircheisen, who delegated the case to the Berlin criminal court and appointed Hoffmann as judge. Hoffmann, perceiving the manifest injustice of the case againt Chézy but obliged to remain neutral, interrogated her three times and managed, by asking what she gratefully recalled as 'masterly and intelligent questions' (H VI, 1505), to prove that she could not have intended to insult the commission.[23] The case against her was dismissed.

Hoffmann and the 'Demagogues'

Hoffmann's sense of justice and his integrity were tested still more severely when he was required to assist in the government's crackdown on supposedly subversive organizations. This necessitates a brief look at the wider political history which Hoffmann preferred to ignore so long as he could. After the defeat of Napoleon, European politics were reorganized under the supervision of Prince Metternich (1773–1859), foreign minister of Austria and from 1821 its chancellor. At the Congress of Vienna in 1815, Metternich began setting up the German Confederation, a loose association of 39 German states, including Austria and Prussia, designed to lay the ghost of the French Revolution by preserving stability and forestalling any demands for more political representation. This ultra-conservative policy disappointed those who had taken up arms against Napoleon in the hope of weakening the power of the German princes, unifying Germany and achieving constitutional government.

Those most severely disillusioned were the members of student fraternities (*Burschenschaften*), enthusiastic German patriots who went about in 'Old German' costume, wore their hair long, sang nationalist anthems and practised gymnastics.[24] Their mentor was the eccentric teacher Friedrich Ludwig Jahn (1778–1852), nicknamed 'Turnvater' (Father of Gymnastics), who advocated a united Germany with a capital, called Teutona, right at its geographical centre. On 18 October 1817, the anniversary of Napoleon's defeat in the Battle of Leipzig, they held a great festival at the Wartburg, where Luther had been imprisoned three centuries earlier. These activities worried the authorities, whose fears seemed justified when on 23 March 1819 the student Karl Sand stabbed to death the playwright August von Kotzebue, an outspoken reactionary and agent of the Russian government. Although Sand also stabbed himself, he recovered from his wounds and was executed on 20 May. Panic ensued. Sand's action was imagined to proceed from a nationwide conspiracy spearheaded by radical groups at the universities of Giessen and Jena. Metternich responded by holding a meeting with other German leaders at Karlsbad in Bohemia to formulate a set of decrees, which were ratified shortly afterwards by the Federal Diet. Universities were placed under strict supervision. Lecturers had to submit the text of their lectures ahead of time. All political meetings were prohibited. The press was strictly censored. People suspected of subversive views were known as 'demagogues' (*Demagogen*). They were arrested on the slightest suspicion and had their correspondence seized.[25]

This political reaction was felt with full force in Hoffmann's Prussia. King Frederick William III revoked his earlier promise to grant a constitution and would permit no representative bodies higher than provincial assemblies. A special government commission was set up to investigate supposed subversion, and Hoffmann, as a senior judge, was made a member. The commission was subject to a higher ministerial commission controlled by the reactionary statesman Prince Wittgenstein and his assistant Karl Albert von Kamptz, director of the Berlin police.

Hoffmann was not happy about his new role. He made his feelings clear in a letter to his old friend Hippel. He disapproved of the young demagogues but thought it wrong to punish them for opinions that did not lead to action:

> At this very time I was appointed to the commission established to investigate the so-called 'demagogic machinations' and, knowing me as you do, you can imagine how I felt when before

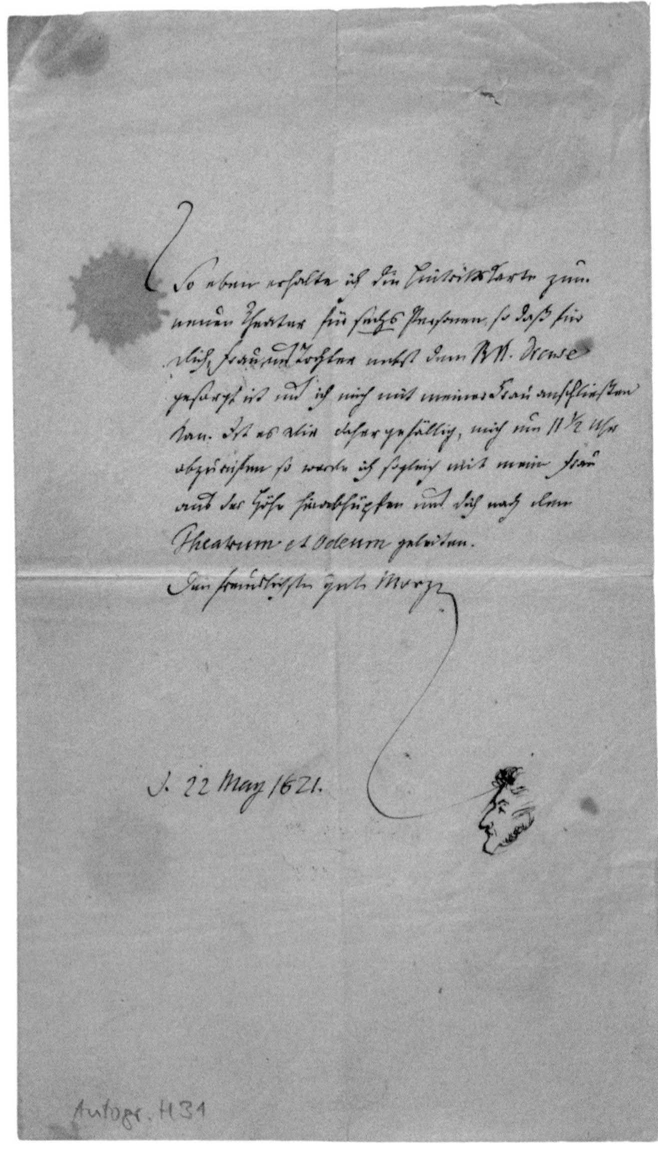

Letter from E.T.A. Hoffmann to Theodor Gottlieb Hippel, 22 May 1821, with a self-portrait in place of a signature.

> my eyes a whole network of uncontrolled licence, impudent disregard for all the laws, personal animosity, emerged! – I need not tell you that like any other fair-minded and truly patriotic man I was and am convinced that an end must be put to the brainsick activities of some young hotheads, especially as these activities were beginning to enter into real life . . . It was time to take legal measures to punish and control with all due severity. Instead, however, measures were taken which were directed not only against deeds, but against opinions [*Gesinnungen*]. (24 June 1820)

One of those accused, Ludwig Roediger, had attracted the authorities' attention by delivering a speech at the Wartburg assembly. Hoffmann noted that though Roediger was clearly discontented with the present state of things, 'this discontentment cannot in itself be imputed to him as a crime deserving punishment' (H VI, 844). Another, August Follenius, had undertaken a political action by distributing a songbook with the alleged purpose of rousing people to oppose the current political order; but that fell far short of high treason (H VI, 806).[26] The inspirer of the *Burschenschaften*, Jahn, came before the commission, accused of subversive plans and incendiary utterances. He wanted Germany to become a republic and for it to be protected against foreign enemies by having its frontiers converted into an artificial wilderness guarded by hungry wolves and bears (H VI, 1046). These were self-evidently absurd fantasies. In response to a leading question, Jahn had affirmed that it would be right to kill Kamptz. But this, Hoffmann pointed out, showed only that Jahn was an immoral person, not that he had any definite plan to commit murder (H VI, 1038–9). Although Hoffmann argued that Jahn should be set free, after prolonged debates he was condemned to imprisonment in a fortress.

By recommending lenient penalties, or none, and by refusing to condemn people merely for opinions, however repellent, Hoffmann infuriated the ministerial commission, especially Kamptz. The latter insisted that there was ample evidence to convict the demagogues of treason and did his best to pressure Hoffmann's commission into changing its judgements.[27] Foiled, he took his revenge later. In December 1821 Hoffmann inserted into *Master Flea*, then with his publisher in Frankfurt, an episode involving one Knarrpanti, a court councillor (*Hofrat*), who demands that Peregrinus Tyss be arrested. When told that no crime has been committed, Knarrpanti 'observed that once the culprit had been identified, the crime would follow automatically' (GP 298). Peregrinus is arrested and his papers are confiscated. Knarrpanti finds evidence of his villainy in such diary entries as 'Today I only killed time.' 'The word "killed" was underlined three times, and Knarrpanti asked whether anyone could reveal his criminal inclinations more clearly than by regretting that on a given day he had killed nothing but time!' (GP 313). This detail is taken from Kamptz's investigations (the word in the original is *mordfaul*, literally 'murder-lazy', that is, bone idle). While the book was in press, Hoffmann got cold feet and asked his publisher in January 1822 to remove some passages that he said could be maliciously misinterpreted. But it was already too late. Kamptz, having heard rumours about the story, sent an agent to question the publisher and confiscate Hoffmann's manuscript and other documents. Hoffmann's letter requesting excisions thus came to light and served to incriminate him.

Hoffmann was now in very serious trouble. Friedrich von Schuckmann, minister of the interior, sent a full account, drafted by Kamptz, to the chancellor, Hardenberg (A 630–33): by using confidential material from government files for malicious and libellous satire, Hoffmann had violated his oath of office and revealed himself as a 'disobedient, thoroughly unreliable and even dangerous state official' (letter of 4 February 1822, A 632). Although Hoffmann deserved to be dismissed from state service, the most feasible as well as appropriate punishment, Schuckmann suggested, would be to transfer him to a remote provincial town such as Insterburg (which, as it happened, was not far from Hoffmann's birthplace, Königsberg). However, Hoffmann's health was breaking down. Thanks to a medical certificate, he was allowed to submit a written defence. He composed a long and disingenuous apologia in which he denied any intention of alluding to Kamptz's activities and asserted that the Knarrpanti episode had been included only to comply with the structural demands of fiction by providing his hero with a suitably unintelligent antagonist. By then, however, Hoffmann was so ill that proceedings against him were suspended. *Master Flea* appeared without the offending passages, which were not found until 1906, and Kamptz went from strength to strength, finally serving for ten years (1832–42) as minister of justice.

Hoffmann's conduct – apart from the unconvincing evasions to which his indiscretion made him resort – testifies to his liberal principles and to his courage in maintaining them under severe official pressure. Far from sympathizing with the beliefs of the demagogues, he deplored their view that their convictions entitled them to override the law. But since they had not actually broken the law, they should not be persecuted for holding opinions that only *might* lead them to do so. His display of *Zivilcourage* (courageous public spirit) should stand beside that shown by the 'Göttingen Seven': the liberal professors at Göttingen University, including the brothers Jacob and Wilhelm Grimm, who in 1837 relinquished their posts rather than take an illegal personal oath of loyalty to their sovereign.

Hoffmann the Invalid

By January 1822 Hoffmann was terminally ill. He had suffered bouts of serious illness before, in the spring of 1818 and 1819. In autumn 1821 he suffered liver failure and a paralysis that gradually spread to his legs and hands. He celebrated his 46th birthday on 26 January with friends, but, as Hitzig recalls, not as before:

> He drank Seltzer water while offering his friends the most exquisite wines, and though on previous such occasions he had circled the table with indefatigable liveliness, filling glasses and animating the conversation whenever it paused, he now spent the whole evening chained to his armchair. (A 623)

In this condition Hoffmann dictated his story about a dying man, 'My Cousin's Corner Window'. The 'cousin' is based on Hoffmann himself. The narrator is a well-meaning but obtuse relative who pays him a visit and finds that the invalid cannot even move between his armchair and his bed without the aid of a surly ex-soldier who nurses him (there is no counterpart to Mischa in the story). Unable to write, the cousin finds relief from depression in watching the bustle of the marketplace beneath his window (Hoffmann's flat, it will be remembered, overlooked the Gendarmenmarkt in the centre of Berlin). Here the cousin has developed the 'art of looking', which he teaches to his visitor. He watches the shoppers and speculates about their lives and characters, drawing plausible inferences from their peculiarities. A fashionably dressed young woman has incongruous footwear, a pair of dancing shoes; from this the cousin deduces that she belongs to the ballet. The two men watch her getting into conversation with a student; the two help each other to select fruit, clearly beginning to form a relationship. Instructing his visitor, the cousin seems to anticipate Sherlock Holmes, who can amaze Dr Watson by deducing from the unbrushed state of a hat that its owner's wife has ceased to love him. This form of knowledge, drawn from clues visible only to the keen observer, has been called by Carlo Ginzburg 'divinatory'. Ginzburg traces it back to the activity of the hunter who learns to read the tracks of animals and contrasts it with the activity of the physical scientist, for whom the object of his knowledge is abstract, quantifiable and indefinitely repeatable. The doctor who 'reads' symptoms, the art connoisseur who attributes paintings and the literary critic all resemble the detective in practising a form of knowledge that cannot be reduced to rules but must be passed on by oral instruction, as the cousin instructs his visitor.[28]

In this story Hoffmann has also given a memorable image of the artist. The artist is cut off from everyday life. But he does not compensate for his isolation by escaping into romantic visions. It is precisely everyday life that interests him, and for which he yearns. His estrangement from everyday life gives him insights into it which he could not have had if he were immersed in it like the rest of us. This kind of artist anticipates Thomas Mann's *Tonio Kröger* (1903), whose hero admits that he is at heart a bourgeois who has lost his way and who appreciates all the more keenly 'the bliss of ordinariness' because he cannot share it.

Hoffmann's friends report that despite his worsening paralysis he retained his spirits and was able to make his countless hardships into amusing stories. He would recount how his muscular attendant threw him into the bath like a piece of wood, and how his maid would then take him in her arms like a child and carry him to bed (A 659). He even endured uncomplainingly the extraordinary attempts by his doctors to reduce his paralysis by applying red-hot irons to his back. On the morning of 25 June, as Hitzig recalls, the wounds made by this procedure began to bleed. This was taken as a portent of imminent death. Hoffmann talked of completing another story, but soon his death rattle set in, and sometime between 10 and 11 a.m., he died (A 662–3).

5

Hoffmann's Literary Afterlife

Hoffmann's reputation since his death has been unstable. During and just after his lifetime, he was seen primarily as a writer of horror fiction. In Britain, this judgement seemed confirmed by the publication in 1824 of *The Devil's Elixirs*, translated by the Edinburgh man of letters Robert Pearse Gillies (1789–1858). It was in the same month that James Hogg (1770–1835) brought out *The Private Memoirs and Confessions of a Justified Sinner*, whose protagonist, like Medardus, is pursued by a malevolent double. The resemblances are close enough to justify the speculation that Hogg had seen Gillies's text before its publication.[1]

Hoffmann's British reputation, however, was severely damaged by another Edinburgh writer, Sir Walter Scott (1771–1832), who in 1827 published an essay on the supernatural in fiction. This work treated Hoffmann, with particular reference to 'The Entail' and 'The Sandman', as a pathological case:

> It is impossible to subject tales of this nature to criticism. They are not the visions of a poetical mind, they have scarcely even the seeming authenticity which the hallucinations of lunacy convey to the patient; they are the feverish dreams of a light-headed patient, to which, though they may sometimes excite by their peculiarity, or surprise by their oddity, we never feel disposed to yield more than momentary attention.[2]

Scott's criticism – perhaps a way of disavowing the supernatural element in his own earlier fiction, particularly his novel

The Antiquary (1816) – was echoed by Goethe, who translated excerpts from the essay with approving comments.[3] Between them, Scott and Goethe seriously harmed Hoffmann's literary standing in both Britain and Germany.

In Russia and France, however, Hoffmann found many appreciative readers and had a lasting resonance. Russian readers soon had access to both Russian and French translations. Enthusiasm for Hoffmann peaked in the 1830s. The contrast of fantastic events in an urban setting, as in Hoffmann's 'The Choosing of the Bride' and other stories set in Berlin, inspired Nikolai Gogol to set such fantastic tales as 'The Nose' (1836) in St Petersburg (a city little more than a century old). Readers seem to have responded especially to *The Devil's Elixirs* and the theme of the double. The terror aroused in Medardus by his double Viktorin afflicts the hapless Golyadkin in Fyodor Dostoevsky's *The Double* (1846). Charles Passage, who has rightly or wrongly detected innumerable motifs borrowed from Hoffmann by Russian writers, argues that the devout Alyosha and the atheist Ivan in *The Brothers Karamazov* (1879–80) complement each other as doubles, and that if Dostoevsky had continued the novel Alyosha would have imitated Medardus by a worldly career of sin and repentance.[4]

Hoffmann's works, especially *The Devil's Elixirs* and 'The Sandman', are major tributaries of the enormous stream of Gothic fantasy in modern literature and cinema.[5] It is perhaps a pity that less attention has been given to the playful Hoffmann of *The Golden Pot, Princess Brambilla* and *Murr*. In France, where several different translations soon became available, Hoffmann enjoyed a vogue from roughly 1820 to 1840 as the author of fantastic tales and as an artist with insight into a transcendent world.[6] Charles Baudelaire (1821–1867), however, had the most original response. Given his interest in altered states induced by intoxication, it is hardly surprising that he singled out for praise a passage in *Fantasy-Pieces* where Hoffmann recommends different drinks to accompany different types of music: champagne for a comic opera, Rhine wine for church music, Burgundy for heroic opera.[7] He is particularly perceptive when he applies to Hoffmann a distinction between kinds of comedy. One is the superficial comedy arising from people's appearance and behaviour (the 'comique significatif'); the other is 'absolute comedy', in which laughter is an expression of humanity's superiority to nature: 'the laughter caused by the grotesque has in itself something profound, axiomatic and primitive which comes much closer to innocent life and absolute joy than does the laughter caused by comedy of manners.'[8] Hoffmann, especially in *Princess Brambilla*, combines both, letting us see how Giglio Fava alternates between his real identity as an actor and his imaginary identity as an Assyrian prince who despises the wretched player Giglio.[9] Baudelaire is responding to the superior position within the narrative of the Prince of Pistoia, alias Celionati, who stage-manages the action and is aware that he and the other characters exist in a work of fiction (see *GP* 237).

Hoffmann's tales also inspired composers. Richard Wagner found material in two stories of Hoffmann's that are set, uncharacteristically for the writer, in earlier periods of German history. The medieval poets in the short story 'The Singers' Contest' helped to inspire *Tannhäuser* (1845), while the novella 'Meister Martin der Küfner und seine Gesellen' ('Master Martin the Cooper and His Journeymen', 1819), a realistic narrative set in 1580 amid the rich historical associations of Nuremberg, contributed to the atmosphere of *Die Meistersinger von Nürnberg* (1868). However, it was Jacques Offenbach (1819–1880) who, with his only opera, *The Tales of Hoffmann* (premiered in 1881, four months after Offenbach's death), did most to sustain Hoffmann's posthumous reputation and shape (misleadingly) his image for posterity. The libretto by the prolific playwright and poet Jules Barbier (1825–1901) presents Hoffmann as the central character. The prologue and epilogue show him drinking with students in a tavern in Nuremberg and torn between his attraction to a prima donna and the claims of art. Each of the three acts adapts a story by Hoffmann, making Hoffmann himself the protagonist. In the first, he falls for the automaton Olimpia (from 'The Sandman'); in the second, he is in love with the doomed Antonia, daughter of the counsellor Crespel (*sic*); and in the third he gives up his mirror image to the courtesan Giulietta, as Erasmus

Spikher does in *Fantasy-Pieces*. After these disastrous experiences, it is not surprising that Hoffmann rejects the prima donna and devotes himself to art. Offenbach's opera perpetuated the image of Hoffmann as a Romantic artist, his imagination fuelled by alcohol, doomed to seek in art a substitute for the happiness that life persists in denying him.

Hoffmann's fiction also provided material for two well-known nineteenth-century ballets. *Coppélia* (1870), composed by Léo Delibes (1836–1891), turns 'The Sandman' into a humorous drama in which the hero confuses the life-size doll Coppélia, made by the toy-maker Professor Coppélius, with his lover Svanilde. 'The Nutcracker and the Mouse-King' provided Pyotr Ilyich Tchaikovsky (1840–1893) with the outline of the two-act ballet *The Nutcracker* (1892), in which the Nutcracker, having killed the Mouse-King in the first act, travels in the second with the heroine to the realm of the Sugar Plum Fairy. Both respond to Hoffmann's comic inventiveness more than to his sinister side.

In the twentieth century, Hoffmann provided a witness to the autonomy of the imagination when it was under threat. In 1921 a group of writers calling themselves the Serapion Brothers was formed in Petrograd (soon to become Leningrad). They included Yevgeny Zamyatin (1884–1937), who had just published the dystopian novel *We*. Its members supported the Revolution, but did not want to see art harnessed to political and practical ends. In 1924 the group issued a manifesto, which announced: 'We believe that literary chimeras are a separate reality, and we oppose utilitarianism. We do not write propaganda. Art is as real as life. And like life, art has no goal or meaning: it exists because it cannot not exist.'[10] These sentiments were unlikely to find favour in the Soviet Union. Members of the group were ignored or denounced; *We* was banned. The group dissolved in 1926.

The Life and Opinions of the Tomcat Murr has had its own afterlife in a strand of fiction in which a cat satirizes the human world. George Eliot (Mary Ann/Marian Evans, 1819–1880) hints at the possibility in *Middlemarch* (1872), just after the heroine has been unexpectedly criticized by her normally docile sister: 'Who can tell what just criticisms Murr the Cat may be passing on us beings of wider speculation?'[11] Although Eliot did not develop this hint, a cat-narrator was used by the Japanese novelist Natsume Sōseki (1867–1916), who was familiar with Western literature. Sōseki alludes briefly to Hoffmann's *Murr* late in his novel *I Am a Cat* (1905–6), in which an unnamed cat comments satirically on the foibles of his owner's intellectual friends and briefly encounters the ghost of 'some German mog called Kater Murr'.[12] The title conveys the feline narrator's self-importance by using a highly formal version of the first-person pronoun.[13] A professed descendant of Murr appears as the narrator of Christa Wolf's (1929–2011) short story 'Neue Lebensansichten eines Katers' ('New Life and Opinions of a Tomcat', 1970), which uses the cat's sceptical perspective for a heavy-handed satire on misguided scientific projects.[14] One can surmise Murr's presence behind the much more readable novels by the Turkish-German writer Akif Pirinçci (1959–), beginning with *Felidae* (1989), which amusingly depict the contempt of the cat Francis for his chaotic owner but also lament the sufferings that the human race inflicts on animals.[15]

At present, Hoffmann's place in the literary canon is secure, and his works, both in German and in English translation, are readily available and widely popular.[16] Yet, although a superb edition of his works has appeared in a series devoted to German classic texts, the word 'classic' does not feel quite right. A classic often induces a feeling of respect tinged with boredom, and Hoffmann is rarely if ever boring. His works are too much fun to fit easily into the pantheon of classics.

References

1 From Königsberg to Berlin, from Music to Literature

1 All available information is collected in Friedrich Schnapp, 'Hoffmanns Brüder', *MHG*, 19 (1973), pp. 52–60.

2 See *Murr*, pp. 69–71. The trumpet marine, not actually a trumpet but a string instrument with one string, played with a bow, is described at length, p. 71.

3 See Jack Zipes, 'Introduction: E.T.A. Hoffmann, the Wounded Storyteller', in *The Wounded Storyteller: The Traumatic Tales of E.T.A. Hoffmann*, trans. Jack Zipes (New Haven, CT, 2023), pp. xiv–xxiii.

4 See Rüdiger Safranski, *E.T.A. Hoffmann: Das Leben eines skeptischen Phantasten* (Munich, 1984), pp. 45–6.

5 Theodor in 'The Entail' reads *The Ghost-Seer* (*Tales*, p. 192); in *The Devil's Elixirs* Aurelie sees a copy of *The Monk* (*DE*, p. 186).

6 See the tribute to Novalis in H II/1, 173.

7 Gerhard Allroggen, 'Der Komponist E.T.A. Hoffmann', H II/2, 705–33 (p. 706). All Hoffmann's known works are listed in Gerhard Allroggen, *E.T.A. Hoffmanns Kompositionen: Ein chronologisch-thematisches Verzeichnis seiner musikalischen Werke mit einer Einführung* (Regensburg, 1970). For surveys of Hoffmann's musical career, see Friedrich Schnapp, 'Der Musiker E.T.A. Hoffmann', *MHG*, 25 (1979), pp. 3–23, and Allroggen's article 'E.T.A. Hoffmann', in *The New Grove Dictionary of Music and Musicians*, ed. Stanley Sadie, 2nd edn, 29 vols (London, 2001), vol. XI, pp. 585–94. For detailed analysis of Hoffmann's compositions, see the essay marking the centenary of his death by Erwin Kroll, 'Über den Musiker E.T.A. Hoffmann: Zur hundertsten Wiederkehr seines Todestages', in *E.T.A. Hoffmann* (Wege der Forschung), ed. Helmut Prang (Darmstadt, 1976), pp. 89–121 (first published in *Zeitschrift für Musikwissenschaft*, 4 (October 1921–September 1922),

pp. 530–52); Werner Keil, *E.T.A. Hoffmann als Komponist: Studien zur Kompositionstechnik an ausgewählten Werken* (Wiesbaden, 1986).

8 Allroggen, H II/2, 725; see Schnapp, 'Der Musiker', p. 8.

9 John Warrack, *German Opera: From the Beginnings to Wagner* (Cambridge, 2001), p. 250.

10 Safranski, *E.T.A. Hoffmann*, p. 170.

11 See Ritchie Robertson, 'Calderón's European Reception from Romanticism to the Twentieth Century', in *A Companion to Calderón de la Barca*, ed. Roy Norton and Jonathan Thacker (Woodbridge, 2021), pp. 284–99.

12 Ronald Taylor, *Hoffmann* (Cambridge, 1963), p. 65; see also p. 34.

13 Allroggen, H II/2, 704–5; Safranski, *E.T.A. Hoffmann*, p. 197.

14 Safranski, *E.T.A. Hoffmann*, pp. 239–40.

15 Keil, *E.T.A. Hoffmann als Komponist*, p. 305.

16 Ibid., p. 307.

17 Quoted by Allroggen, 'E.T.A. Hoffmann', p. 590.

18 R. Murray Schafer, *E.T.A. Hoffmann and Music* (Toronto, 1975), p. 179; Keil, *E.T.A. Hoffmann als Komponist*, p. 158. For the influence of Mozart's symphony see Kroll, 'Über den Musiker E.T.A. Hoffmann', p. 102.

19 Schafer, *E.T.A. Hoffmann and Music*, p. 180.

20 Kroll, 'Über den Musiker E.T.A. Hoffmann', p. 102.

21 See Robin Wallace, *Beethoven's Critics: Aesthetic Dilemmas and Resolutions during the Composer's Lifetime* (Cambridge, 1986), p. 26.

22 Wilhelm Heinrich Wackenroder, *Dichtungen, Schriften, Briefe*, ed. Gerda Heinrich (Berlin, 1984), p. 162.

23 Jean le Rond d'Alembert, 'Discours préliminaire de l'Encyclopédie', in *Œuvres complètes de d'Alembert*, 5 vols (Paris, 1821), vol. I, p. 39.

24 Immanuel Kant, *Critique of the Power of Judgment*, in *The Cambridge Edition of the Works of Immanuel Kant*, trans. Paul Guyer, ed. Paul Guyer and Eric Matthews (Cambridge, 2000), p. 206.

25 H III, 460; Hoffmann is quoting from the essay 'Über die Begeisterung des Künstlers', in Carl Ludwig Fernow, *Römische Studien*, vol. I (Zurich, 1806), pp. 255–78.

26 'Letter from Milo, an educated ape, to his lady-friend Pipi in North America', C 137–44 (p. 141).

27 See Victoria Dutchman-Smith, *E.T.A. Hoffmann and Alcohol: Biography, Reception and Art* (Leeds, 2010), esp. ch. 1.

28 See especially the articles on Hoffmann by John M. Ellis, cited liberally throughout this book and listed in the Bibliography.

29 Review of Gluck's *Iphigénie en Aulide*, 1810, in C 256–62.

30 See Gluck's dedication to *Alceste*, quoted in Ricarda Schmidt, *Wenn mehrere Künste im Spiel sind: Intermedialität bei E.T.A. Hoffmann* (Göttingen, 2006), p. 26.
31 See Schmidt, *Wenn mehrere Künste im Spiel sind*, p. 60.
32 Wolfgang Nehring, 'E.T.A. Hoffmanns Erzählwerk: ein Modell und seine Variationen', *Zeitschrift für deutsche Philologie*, 95 (1976), pp. 3–24 (p. 22). On the reception of Hoffmann's story, see also Warrack, *German Opera*, pp. 278–81.
33 See Richard Eldridge, '"Hidden Secrets of the Self": E.T.A. Hoffmann's Reading of *Don Giovanni*', in *The Don Giovanni Moment: Essays on the Legacy of an Opera*, ed. Lydia Goehr and Daniel Herwitz (New York, 2006), pp. 33–46 (esp. pp. 38–40).
34 On *Der Trank der Unsterblichkeit*, see the appreciation by Warrack, *German Opera*, pp. 250–51. The opera was not performed until 2012.
35 For a summary of *Aurora*, see C 183.
36 See Hoffmann's diary, H I, 428, and the account by Kunz, A 208.
37 See Wulf Segebrecht, *Autobiographie und Dichtung: Eine Studie zum Werk E.T.A. Hoffmanns* (Stuttgart, 1967), p. 107.
38 For an ingenious argument that these events reappear in the mechanical horrors of 'The Sandman', see John Zilcosky, 'Hoffmann at the Battle of Dresden: "The Sandman" and the Napoleonic Wars', in *The Language of Trauma: War and Technology in Hoffmann, Freud, and Kafka* (Toronto, 2021), pp. 17–40.
39 'Extremely Random Thoughts', C 111; H II/1, 69.
40 See the diary entries for 1813, quoted in Safranski, *E.T.A. Hoffmann*, p. 285.

2 Bamberg: Medicine, Psychology and Fiction

1 On animal magnetism, see Matthew Bell, *The German Tradition of Psychology in Literature and Thought, 1700–1840* (Cambridge, 2005), ch. 6.
2 Henri F. Ellenberger, *The Discovery of the Unconscious: The History and Evolution of Dynamic Psychiatry* (London, 1970), pp. 62–3.
3 H IV, 324. See Aldous Huxley, *The Devils of Loudun* (London, 1952); Ken Russell's film about these events, *The Devils* (1971); and generally Brian P. Levack, *The Devil Within: Possession and Exorcism in the Christian West* (New Haven, CT, and London, 2013). In the late nineteenth century, Jean-Marie Charcot made his hysterical patients display their symptoms publicly at the Salpêtrière hospital, where they were

witnessed by Freud: see Mark Micale, *Approaching Hysteria: Disease and Its Interpretations* (Princeton, NJ, 1995), pp. 25–8; and generally Ellenberger, *The Discovery of the Unconscious*.

4 See Iain McCalman, *The Seven Ordeals of Count Cagliostro* (London, 2003).

5 These connections are explored in Michael Rohrwasser, *Coppelius, Cagliostro und Napoleon: Der verborgene politische Blick E.T.A. Hoffmanns* (Basel and Frankfurt, 1991).

6 F.W.J. Schelling, 'Von der Weltseele', in *Schellings Werke*, ed. Manfred Schröter, vol. I (Munich, 1927), pp. 413–651 (p. 458); see also p. 474.

7 Helpful introductions to Schubert are Hans J. Hahn, 'G. H. Schubert's Principle of Untimely Development (Aspects of Schubert's *Ansichten von der Nachtseite der Naturwissenschaft* and Its Reverberations in Romantic Literature)', *German Life and Letters*, XXXVII/4 (1984), pp. 336–53, and Bell, *The German Tradition of Psychology*, pp. 170–72.

8 Gotthilf Heinrich Schubert, *Ansichten von der Nachtseite der Naturwissenschaften* (Dresden, 1808), pp. 359–60.

9 See M. H. Abrams, *Natural Supernaturalism: Tradition and Revolution in Romantic Literature* (New York, 1971), esp. ch. 4, with German examples including Goethe, Novalis and Kleist.

10 This qualifies the – otherwise broadly convincing – contrast drawn by Karl Ludwig Schneider, 'Künstlerliebe und Philistertum im Werk E.T.A. Hoffmanns', in *Die deutsche Romantik: Poetik, Formen und Motive*, ed. Hans Steffen (Göttingen, 1967), pp. 200–218.

11 The story is divided not into chapters but into vigils, implying that it was written during a succession of sleepless nights.

12 See John Reddick, 'E.T.A. Hoffmann's *Der Goldne Topf* and Its "durchgehaltene Ironie"', *Modern Language Review*, LXXI/3 (1976), pp. 577–94.

13 See Jürgen Barkhoff, *Magnetische Fiktionen: Literarisierung des Mesmerismus in der Romantik* (Stuttgart and Weimar, 1995), p. 217.

14 See the detailed but one-dimensional interpretation by Friedhelm Auhuber, *In einem fernen dunklen Spiegel: E.T.A. Hoffmanns Poetisierung der Medizin* (Opladen, 1986), pp. 36–54. A concise but comprehensive reading, integrating psychological data and acknowledging the story's multivalence, is offered in Bell, *The German Tradition of Psychology*, pp. 200–204.

15 Goethe makes Faust invoke elemental spirits in *Faust*, Part I, ll. 1282–91, drawing on Agrippa and Paracelsus: see the commentary in Johann Wolfgang Goethe, *Sämtliche Werke: Briefe, Tagebücher und Gespräche*,

ed. Friedmar Apel et al., 40 vols (Frankfurt, 1986–2000), vol. VII/2, pp. 248–9. The abbé Villars de Montfaucon elaborated this mythology in *Le Comte de Gabalis, ou Entretiens des sciences secrètes* (Paris, 1670), which provided Alexander Pope with the mythological apparatus of *The Rape of the Lock* (1714).

16 James M. McGlathery, 'The Suicide Motif in E.T.A. Hoffmann's *Der goldne Topf*', *Monatshefte*, LVIII/2 (1966), pp. 115–23; Auhuber, *In einem fernen dunklen Spiegel*, p. 40.

17 Against gloomy interpretations like McGlathery's, I much prefer the utopian reading suggested by Jack Zipes, 'Introduction: E.T.A. Hoffmann, the Wounded Storyteller', in *The Wounded Storyteller: The Traumatic Tales of E.T.A. Hoffmann*, trans. Jack Zipes (New Haven, CT, 2023), pp. xiv–xxiii.

18 Wolfgang Nehring, 'E.T.A. Hoffmanns Erzählwerk: ein Modell und seine Variationen', in his *Spätromantiker: Eichendorff und E.T.A. Hoffmann* (Göttingen, 1997), pp. 119–41 (p. 126).

19 S. S. Prawer, 'Hoffmann's Uncanny Guest: A Reading of *Der Sandmann*', *German Life and Letters*, XVIII/4 (1965), pp. 297–308 (p. 302).

20 See John M. Ellis, 'Clara, Nathanael, and the Narrator: Interpreting Hoffmann's *Der Sandmann*', *German Quarterly*, LIV/1 (1981), pp. 1–18.

21 Documented by Auhuber, *In einem fernen dunklen Spiegel*, pp. 55–9.

22 Ellis, 'Clara, Nathanael, and the Narrator', p. 8; similarly Bell, *The German Tradition of Psychology*, pp. 204–7.

23 As is done wholesale by Kenneth Negus, *E.T.A. Hoffmann's Other World: The Romantic Author and His 'New Mythology'* (Philadelphia, PA, 1965), p. 91.

24 Stefan Matuschek applies this model to some Romantic texts in *Der gedichtete Himmel: Eine Geschichte der Romantik* (Munich, 2021), pp. 67–86.

25 For the case against Clara, see Ellis, 'Clara, Nathanael, and the Narrator', pp. 9–11.

26 'The Uncanny', in *The Standard Edition of the Complete Psychological Works of Sigmund Freud*, ed. James Strachey, 24 vols (London, 1953–74), vol. XVII, pp. 217–52 (esp. pp. 231–2).

27 See Prawer, 'Hoffmann's Uncanny Guest', p. 302, and for a trenchant critique of Freud's interpretation, Graham Frankland, *Freud's Literary Culture* (Cambridge, 2000), pp. 97–8.

28 Adolph Freiherr von Knigge, *Über den Umgang mit Menschen*, ed. Gert Ueding (Frankfurt, 1977), p. 391. See J. M. Roberts, *The Mythology of the Secret Societies* (London, 1972).

29 Heinrich Heine, *Briefe aus Berlin*, in *Sämtliche Schriften*, ed. Klaus Briegleb, 6 vols (Munich, 1968–76), vol. II, p. 66.

30 Commentators disagree about whether the elixir is actually alcohol, and whether it really changes Medardus's behaviour or simply strengthens the criminal desires already present in him: see Victoria Dutchman-Smith, *E.T.A. Hoffmann and Alcohol: Biography, Reception and Art* (Leeds, 2010), pp. 152–5.

31 The notoriously intricate family relationships are explained, with the help of a diagram, in Kenneth Negus, 'The Family Tree in E.T.A. Hoffmann's *Die Elixiere des Teufels*', *Publications of the Modern Languages Association of America*, LXXIII/5 (1958), pp. 516–20. See also the family tree in H II/2, 392.

32 Elizabeth Wright, *E.T.A. Hoffmann and the Rhetoric of Terror* (London, 1978), p. 165.

33 Commentators inspired by psychoanalysis have inevitably written much about Hoffmann and particularly about *The Devil's Elixirs*, in a tradition going back to Freud's disciple Otto Rank, whose *Der Doppelgänger*, written in 1914 and published in 1925, is available in English as *The Double: A Psychoanalytic Study*, trans. Harry Tucker (Chapel Hill, NC, 1971). See also Ralph Tymms, *Doubles in Literary Psychology* (Cambridge, 1949); Andrew Webber, *The Doppelgänger: Double Visions in German Literature* (Oxford, 1996).

34 For example, Johann Christian Reil, *Rhapsodieen über die Anwendung der psychischen Curmethoden auf Geisteszerrüttungen* (Halle, 1803), pp. 306–64.

35 G. H. Schubert, *Die Symbolik des Traumes* (Bamberg, 1814), p. 119.

36 Walter Hinderer holds an exemplary balance between psychological ideas Hoffmann gained from his reading and later ideas developed by Freud and Jung: 'Die poetische Psychoanalyse in E.T.A. Hoffmanns Roman *Die Elixiere des Teufels*', in *'Hoffmanneske Geschichte': Zu einer Literaturwissenschaft als Kulturwissenschaft*, ed. Gerhard Neumann (Würzburg, 2005), pp. 43–76.

37 See the parallel-text edition, Pedro Calderón de la Barca, *La devoción de la Cruz*/August Wilhelm Schlegel, *Die Andacht zum Kreuz*, ed. Carol Tully, MHRA European Translations, 3 (London, 2012).

38 English translations of *Die Elixere*, even the otherwise excellent one by Ronald Taylor, often tendentiously mistranslate Hoffmann's religious and supernatural vocabulary. See Ritchie Robertson, '"Unerforschliches Verhängnis!" The Vocabulary of "Fate" in English Translations of E.T.A. Hoffmann's *Die Elixiere des Teufels*', *Studi Germanici*, 25 (2024), pp. 69–92.

39 Heine in *The Romantic School and Other Essays*, ed. Jost Hermand and Robert C. Holub, trans. Helen Mustard et al. (New York, 1985), p. 76.

40 Ibid.

3 Hoffmann the Storyteller

1 The drawing, which is very large, can be found between pages 66 and 67 of Hoffmann, *Briefwechsel*, ed. Hans von Müller and Friedrich Schnapp, vol. II (Munich, 1968). It is also reproduced on a smaller scale, but accompanied by a detailed explanation, in Rüdiger Safranski, *E.T.A. Hoffmann: Das Leben eines skeptischen Phantasten* (Munich, 1984), pp. 492–6. Sections of the drawing are reproduced in H II/2, after p. 544.

2 Safranski, *E.T.A. Hoffmann*, p. 383.

3 Victoria Dutchman-Smith, *E.T.A. Hoffmann and Alcohol: Biography, Reception and Art* (Leeds, 2010).

4 *Absalom and Achitophel*, ll. 156–7, in *The Poems and Fables of John Dryden*, ed. James Kinsley (London, 1962), p. 194.

5 Kenneth Negus, *E.T.A. Hoffmann's Other World: The Romantic Author and His 'New Mythology'* (Philadelphia, PA, 1965), p. 81.

6 See Wolfgang Preisendanz, *Humor als dichterische Einbildungskraft* (Munich, 1963), who notes (p. 50 n.) that Hoffmann takes the word 'duality' or 'doubleness' (*Duplizität*) from the satirist Georg Christoph Lichtenberg: Lichtenberg, *Schriften und Briefe*, ed. Wolfgang Promies, 4 vols (Munich, 1967–72), vol. I, p. 813. Here and in his essay 'Daß du auf dem Blocksberg wärst' (1799) Lichtenberg tells the story of the dual crown prince that Hoffmann borrows in *Princess Brambilla* (GP 223–4).

7 Elucidated at length in Hilda Meldrum Brown, *E.T.A. Hoffmann and the Serapiontic Principle: Critique and Creativity* (Rochester, NY, 2006).

8 See M. H. Abrams, *Natural Supernaturalism: Tradition and Revolution in Romantic Literature* (New York, 1971), pp. 179–87 and *passim*; for the application of this model to Hoffmann, Brown, *E.T.A. Hoffmann and the Serapiontic Principle*, pp. 36–7.

9 'Über die Aufführung der Schauspiele des Calderon de la Barca auf dem Theater in Bamberg', H II/1, 625–30 (p. 628).

10 Krespel is based on a real person, Johann Bernhard Crespel, living in Frankfurt, whom Hoffmann probably heard about from Clemens Brentano. Crespel is mentioned in a letter to Goethe from his mother, who says that he made his own trousers and built a house all by

himself to his own design. Crespel's family, offended by Hoffmann's story, insisted that he had been happily married and was a good father (H IV, 1276, 1281).

11 H IV, 54; the comparison with insects is omitted in Hollingdale's translation, see *Tales* 173.

12 John M. Ellis, 'Hoffmann: *Rat Krespel*', in his *Narration in the German Novelle* (Cambridge, 1974), pp. 94–112. This is outstanding as a sensitive and searching analysis.

13 'Le Vrai peut quelquefois n'être pas vraisemblable': Nicolas Boileau-Despréaux, *Épîtres, Art Poétique, Le Lutrin*, ed. Charles-H. Bouhours (Paris, 1952), p. 97.

14 Heinrich von Kleist, *The Marquise von O– and Other Stories*, trans. David Luke and Nigel Reeves (Harmondsworth, 1978), p. 205.

15 *Das nussbraune Mädchen* was published separately in 1816 and was later incorporated into Goethe's novel *Wilhelm Meisters Wanderjahre* (Wilhelm Meister's Journeyman Years), initially published in 1821 with a second edition in 1829.

16 The original is more emphatic: 'das böse Verhängnis, die unheimliche Macht' (H III, 283: 'the evil destiny, the uncanny power'), vocabulary also prominent in *The Devil's Elixirs*.

17 On the historically attested poisonings, see Anne Somerset, *The Affair of the Poisons: Murder, Infanticide and Satanism at the Court of Louis XIV* (London, 2003). Though not essential to the plot, they provide a background of collective panic and equally terrifying police repression, which makes it even harder to clear an unjustly accused person. Hoffmann incorporated material from numerous historical sources, including German translations of Voltaire's *Le Siècle de Louis XIV* and the compendium of true-crime stories *Causes célèbres et intéressantes*, edited by François Gayot de Pitaval, known for short as 'Pitaval'.

18 The English translation is ambiguous: 'I have been told a strange story . . .' (*Tales* 63). The German original makes this clear: 'Von meiner Mutter erzählte man mir eine wunderliche Geschichte' (H IV, 832): 'Someone told me a strange story about my mother.'

19 Kleist, *The Marquise von O– and Other Stories*, p. 114.

20 John M. Ellis, 'E.T.A. Hoffmann's *Das Fräulein von Scuderi*', *Modern Language Review*, LXIV/2 (1969), pp. 340–50 (p. 346). In this paragraph I follow Ellis's interpretation.

21 James Trainer, 'The *Märchen*', in *The Romantic Period in Germany*, ed. Siegbert Prawer (London, 1970), pp. 97–120 (p. 97).

22 'Typical of many of Hoffmann's heroines, [Marie] represents the imaginative spirit of hope that enables her to rebel against traumatization': Jack Zipes, 'Introduction: E.T.A. Hoffmann, the Wounded Storyteller', in *The Wounded Storyteller: The Traumatic Tales of E.T.A. Hoffmann*, trans. Jack Zipes (New Haven, CT, 2023), pp. xiv–xxiii (p. xvii).

23 For a reading of the story in the light of current disability studies, see Eleoma Joshua, 'Misreading the Body: E.T.A. Hoffmann's *Klein Zaches genannt Zinnober*', in *Disability in German Literature, Film, and Theater*, ed. Eleoma Joshua and Michael Schillmeier (Rochester, NY, 2023), pp. 39–56.

24 S. S. Prawer, *Karl Marx and World Literature* (Oxford, 1976), p. 373.

25 Famagusta and Samarkand are the settings for Clemens Brentano's 'Singspiel' *Die lustigen Musikanten* (The Merry Musicians, 1804), which Hoffmann set to music.

26 The doge's name was actually Faliero, as in Byron's play *Marino Faliero* (1821). On the *Liebestod*, see Hartmut Steinecke, *Die Kunst der Fantasie: E.T.A. Hoffmanns Leben und Werk* (Frankfurt, 2004), p. 340. Contemporaries were sharply aware of the real-life *Liebestod* of Heinrich von Kleist and his lover Henriette Vogel.

27 See Brown, *Hoffmann and the Serapiontic Principle*, p. 138.

28 The mines at Falun, now a World Heritage Site, which I visited on 19 April 2024, display a gigantic cavity in the earth, the Stora Stötan or Great Pit, resulting from the collapse of three mine shafts in 1677. Fortunately it was Midsummer Day, the miners were off work and there were no casualties. See 'The Petrified Miner', in Daniels Sven Olsson, *Falun Mine*, trans. Alan Crozier (Falun, 2010), pp. 63–7.

29 The translation I consulted – by Sally Hayward, revised by R. J. Hollingdale – omits much local colour: thus Hoffmann calls the river Götha the 'Göthaelf' (Swedish *älv*, river), an inn a 'Gästgifvaregard' (Swedish *gästgivargård*), and so on. He anticipates criticism by making the story's hearers complain about gratuitous detail (H IV, 239–40).

30 See the comparison of the two stories by Theodore Ziolkowski, *German Romanticism and Its Institutions* (Princeton, NJ, 1990), pp. 51–7.

31 A point made by Steinecke, *Die Kunst der Fantasie*, p. 346.

32 The Itzigs were a well-known Jewish banking family. Heinrich Heine (1797–1856), who himself converted in 1827, recounted Hitzig's change of name humorously in his long poem *Jehuda ben Halevy*: see *The Complete Poems of Heinrich Heine*, trans. Hal Draper (Oxford, 1982), p. 674.

33 See Stefi Jersch-Wenzel, 'Legal Status and Emancipation', in *German-Jewish History in Modern Times*, vol. II: *Emancipation and Assimilation, 1780–1871*, ed. Michael A. Meyer (New York, 1997), pp. 7–49 (esp. pp. 27–38).

34 See the interpretation by Birgit Röder, *A Study of the Major Novellas of E.T.A. Hoffmann* (Rochester, NY, 2003), pp. 105–25.

4 Hoffmann in Berlin, 1814–22

1 See Hoffmann's praise of Gluck in his review of *Iphigénie en Aulide*, published in the *AMZ* on 29 August and 5 September 1810 (C 255–62).

2 Fouqué's story, which is set beside the Danube, is probably indebted to the play by Karl Hensler, *Das Donauweibchen* (The Woman from the Danube, 1798), and the opera based on it by Ferdinand Kauer (1799). Hensler's play was popular throughout Germany (see its mention in *The Golden Pot*, *GP* 4) and was performed even in Denmark, where Hans Christian Andersen saw it as a boy. If so, it may have helped, alongside *Undine*, to shape his story 'Den lille Havfrue' ('The Little Mermaid', 1837). See Otto Rommel, *Das Alt-Wiener Volkstheater* (Vienna, 1952), pp. 559–72 (for Andersen, p. 571). On Andersen and Fouqué, see Paul Binding, *Hans Christian Andersen: European Witness* (New Haven, CT, 2014), who gives a detailed summary of *Undine* (pp. 127–30). On the European popularity of the motif of the seductive water-spirit, see John Warrack, *German Opera: From the Beginnings to Mozart* (Cambridge, 2001), pp. 188–90.

3 See *Goethe: Selected Verse (Penguin Poets)*, ed. and trans. David Luke (Harmondsworth, 1964), p. 79.

4 Warrack, *German Opera*, p. 283.

5 R. Murray Schafer, *E.T.A. Hoffmann and Music* (Toronto, 1975), p. 180.

6 On Goldoni, Chiari and Gozzi, see Peter Brand and Lino Pertile, eds, *The Cambridge History of Italian Literature* (Cambridge, 1996), pp. 355–62.

7 Thomas Cramer, *Das Groteske bei E.T.A. Hoffmann* (Munich, 1966), pp. 142–3. See for example *Mägera, die förchterliche Hexe* (Mägera, the Frightful Witch, 1764), in Philipp Hafner, *Komödien*, ed. Johann Sonnleitner (Vienna, 2001), pp. 81–149. 'Faffner' is supposed by Hoffmann's editor (H I, 1160) to allude to the giant transformed into a dragon in Fouqué's play *Sigurd, der Schlangentöter* (Sigurd, the Serpent-Slayer, 1810), but the grim heroic atmosphere in Fouqué is utterly

unlike Gozzi. On the popularity of Viennese magical plays in south Germany, see Cramer, *Das Groteske*, pp. 152–8.

8 See also 'Der Magnetiseur', where Bickert compares a dream to a Gozzi fairy tale (H II/1, 188); *Seltsame Leiden eines Theater-Direktors*, where the Man in Brown recounts at great length the plot of *Love of Three Oranges* (H III, 507–14); and Berganza's praise of Gozzi (H II/1, 171). In 1809 Hoffmann expressed keen interest in an edition of Gozzi's works that Hitzig was planning to publish in Italian, a language Hoffmann knew well (letter, 25 May 1809).

9 I thank Luciana O'Flaherty of Oxford University Press for permission to reprint, with minor revisions, the interpretation of *Brambilla* published in the 'Introduction' to my translation, *The Golden Pot and Other Tales* (Oxford, 1992), pp. xxiii–xxvi. For introductions to *Brambilla* in English, see Harvey W. Hewett-Thayer, *Hoffmann: Author of the Tales* (Princeton, NJ, 1948), pp. 233–7, and the 'Introduction' to the edition of *Brambilla* by M. M. Raraty (Oxford, 1972), pp. ix–xlix. I found particularly useful Wolfgang Preisendanz, *Humor als dichterische Einbildungskraft* (Munich, 1963), pp. 51–64, and Heide Eilert, *Theater in der Erzählkunst: Eine Studie zum Werk E.T.A. Hoffmanns* (Tübingen, 1977).

10 Reinhold Grimm, 'From Callot to Butor: E.T.A. Hoffmann and the Tradition of the Capriccio', *MLN*, XCIII/3 (1978), pp. 399–415 (p. 400). Although Hoffmann may not have known it, he had an important predecessor in the Enlightenment author C. M. Wieland, who attributes his whimsical verse romance *Idris und Zenide* (1767) to 'the sprite Capriccio': Wieland, 'Vorrede' to *Idris und Zenide*, in his *Werke*, ed. Fritz Martini and Hans Werner Seiffert, 5 vols (Munich, 1964–8), vol. IV, p. 190.

11 Giglio's vanity is all the less excusable since Taer in Gozzi's play is much less heroic than his lover the Princess Dardanè. Taer spends most of the play involuntarily transformed into the titular blue monster, and is restored to human form only through Dardanè's courage. See Carlo Gozzi, *Le Fiabe*, 2 vols (Milan, n.d.), vol. II, pp. 159–236.

12 See Edwin Williamson, 'Miguel de Cervantes (1547–1616): *Don Quixote*: Romance and Picaresque', in *The Cambridge Companion to European Novelists*, ed. Michael Bell (Cambridge, 2012), pp. 17–35 (p. 27).

13 On the quotations and their varied functions, see Herman Meyer, *The Poetics of Quotation in the European Novel*, trans. Yetta Ziolkowski (Princeton, NJ, 1968), pp. 125–47; Ritchie Robertson, 'Shakespearean Comedy and Romantic Psychology in Hoffmann's *Kater Murr*', *Studies in Romanticism*, XXIV/2 (1985), pp. 201–22.

14 See the account of his childhood, with many parallels to Hoffmann's, that Kreisler gives to Master Abraham (*Murr* 72–7).

15 The anonymous text begins, 'Ah che mi manca l'anima in si fatal momento,' 'Ah, that my heart fails me at so fatal a moment.' Hoffmann composed it in 1812 as one of *Six Little Italian Duets for Soprano and Tenor* (note in *Murr* 336; H V, 1021).

16 Walther Harich, in *E.T.A. Hoffmann: Das Leben eines Künstlers*, 2 vols (Berlin, 1920), tried to reconstruct the characters' concealed relationships in the utmost detail and provided a conjectural family tree, including a few characters not mentioned in the novel (vol. II, p. 223). He supposed that the painter Ettlinger was the elder brother of Irenaeus and the father of Kreisler, who was thus the real heir of Sieghartsweiler.

17 Hans von Müller, ed., *Das Kreislerbuch* (Leipzig, 1903).

18 Translation (slightly modified) from Hewett-Thayer, *Hoffmann*, p. 307; original in Hitzig's memoir, A 607.

19 'Frailty, thy name is woman!' – *Hamlet*, I.2.146. Hoffmann, who did not know English, read Shakespeare in the Schlegel–Tieck translation.

20 This contrast is drawn by Hartmut Steinecke, *Die Kunst der Fantasie: E.T.A. Hoffmanns Leben und Werk* (Frankfurt, 2004), pp. 534–5.

21 For example, Friedrich Schiller, 'Der Verbrecher aus verlorener Ehre' (The Criminal of Lost Honour, 1786), in *Schiller's Literary Prose Works*, trans. and ed. Jeffrey L. High (Rochester, NY, 2008).

22 See Chapter Two above; Safranski, *E.T.A. Hoffmann: Das Leben eines skeptischen Phantasten* (Munich, 1984), pp. 425–35.

23 H VI, 1505, quoting Chézy's memoirs; also in A 343–4. Wilhelmine von Chézy was a German noblewoman living apart from her second husband, a professor of Sanskrit in Paris.

24 Heinrich Heine, who disliked the 'demagogues' for their nationalism and antisemitism, gives a hilarious description of one in Chapter Three of his travel book *Reise von München nach Genua* (Journey from Munich to Genoa, 1830) with long hair, open-necked shirt and 'Old German' coat; this figure, in an allusion to James Fenimore Cooper's recently published *The Last of the Mohicans*, is called 'the last of the demagogues'. In *Die Harzreise* (The Harz Journey, 1824) Heine describes nationalist students drinking in the inn on top of the Brocken and singing the patriotic song 'Der Gott, der Eisen wachsen ließ,/ Der wollte keine Knechte' ('The God who planted iron,/ He did not make us slaves'), recordings of which can be found on

YouTube. See Heine, *The Harz Journey and Selected Prose*, trans. Ritchie Robertson, 2nd edn (London, 2006), p. 73.

25 See Christopher Clark, *Iron Kingdom: The Rise and Downfall of Prussia, 1600–1947* (London, 2006), pp. 399–403.

26 Follenius or Follen (1794–1855) should not be confused with his brother the agitator Karl Follen (1795–1840), who published a poetic address to 'the German masses' and fled, first to Switzerland and later to the United States.

27 See for example the appeals by Kamptz printed in Hoffmann, *Juristische Arbeiten*, ed. Friedrich Schnapp (Munich, 1973), pp. 391–4, 490–93.

28 See Carlo Ginzburg, 'Clues: Roots of an Evidential Paradigm', in *Myths, Emblems, Clues*, trans. John and Anne C. Tedeschi (London, 1990), pp. 96–125. I have borrowed some sentences in this paragraph from my 'Introduction' to *The Golden Pot and Other Tales*, pp. xxxi–xxxii.

5 Hoffmann's Literary Afterlife

1 See John Carey's introduction to his edition of the *Confessions* (London, 1969), pp. xxi–xxii.

2 'On the Supernatural in Fictitious Composition, particularly in the Work of Ernest Theodore William Hoffmann', in *Sir Walter Scott on Novelists and Fiction*, ed. Ioan Williams (London, 1968), pp. 312–53 (p. 352). See the important discussion by Barry Murnane, 'Fantastic Histories and Discursive Doubles: Scott, Hoffmann, Alexis and De Quincey', *Angermion*, IX (2016), pp. 1–43.

3 'The Foreign Quarterly Review', in Johann Wolfgang Goethe, *Sämtliche Werke: Briefe, Tagebücher und Gespräche*, ed. Friedmar Apel et al., Deutsche Klassiker-Ausgabe, 40 vols (Frankfurt, 1986–2000), vol. XXII, pp. 709–12.

4 Charles E. Passage, *The Russian Hoffmannists* (The Hague, 1963), pp. 218–19.

5 On film, see S. S. Prawer, *Caligari's Children: The Film as Tale of Terror* (Oxford, 1980).

6 Rosemary Lloyd, *Baudelaire et Hoffmann: Affinités et influences* (Cambridge, 1979), pp. 9–32.

7 See C 112 (= H II/1, 70); Charles Baudelaire, *Œuvres complètes*, ed. Claude Pichois, 2 vols (Paris, 1975), vol. I, p. 378.

8 Charles Baudelaire, 'De l'essence du rire', in *Œuvres complètes*, vol. II, pp. 525–43 (p. 535).

9 Ibid., p. 542.

10 Andrew Kahn et al., *A History of Russian Literature* (Oxford, 2018), pp. 530–31.

11 George Eliot, *Middlemarch* [1872] (Harmondsworth, 1965), p. 60.

12 Sōseki Natsume, *I Am a Cat*, trans. Aiko Itō and Graeme Wilson (Tokyo, 2007), p. 465.

13 See Val Scullion and Marion Treby, 'Feline Affinities between E.T.A. Hoffmann's *The Life and Opinions of the Tomcat Murr* and Natsume Soseki's *I Am a Cat*', *English Language and Literature Studies*, XI/2 (2021), pp. 1–19.

14 See Christa Wolf, *Gesammelte Erzählungen* (Darmstadt, 1981), pp. 97–123.

15 I thank my stepson John Mourby for drawing my attention to Pirinçci's books.

16 My own translation, *The Golden Pot and Other Stories*, has been in print continuously since it appeared in 1992.

Bibliography

This is a list of the literary and musical works by Hoffmann discussed in the text, with references to available translations. Abbreviations are as follows:

Bell *The Nutcracker and The Strange Child*, trans. Anthea Bell (London, 2010)
Bleiler *The Best Tales of Hoffmann*, trans. E. F. Bleiler (New York, 1967)
C *E.T.A. Hoffmann's Musical Writings*, ed. David Charlton and trans. Martyn Clarke (Cambridge, 1989)
GP *The Golden Pot and Other Tales*, trans. Ritchie Robertson (Oxford, 1992)
Tales *Tales of Hoffmann*, trans. R. J. Hollingdale et al. (Harmondsworth, 1982)
Zipes *The Wounded Storyteller: The Traumatic Tales of E.T.A. Hoffmann*, trans. Jack Zipes (New Haven, CT, 2023)

Stories

Included in *Fantasiestücke in Callots Manier* (Fantasy-Pieces in the Manner of Callot), 4 vols (Bamberg, 1814–15):

'Ritter Gluck' ('The Chevalier Gluck', 1809)
'Don Juan' (1812)
Der Goldne Topf (The Golden Pot, 1814), trans. in Bleiler (as *The Golden Flower Pot*), *GP* and Zipes
'Der Magnetiseur' ('The Magnetizer', 1814)
'Der Musikfeind' ('The Music-Hater', 1814), trans. in C

Included in *Nachtstücke* (Night-Pieces), 2 vols (Berlin, 1816–17):

'Nachricht von den neuesten Schicksalen des Hundes Berganza' ('News of the Most Recent Experiences of the Dog Berganza', 1814)
'Die Geschichte vom verlorenen Spiegelbilde' ('The Tale of the Lost Reflection', 1815), trans. in Bleiler as part of 'A New Year's Eve Adventure'
'Ignaz Denner' (1816)
'Die Jesuiterkirche in G–' ('The Jesuit Church in G[logau]', 1816)
'Der Sandmann' ('The Sandman', 1816), trans. in Bleiler, *Tales*, GP and Zipes
'Das Majorat' ('The Entail', 1817), trans. in *Tales*

Included in *Die Serapions-Brüder* (The Serapion Brethren), 4 vols (Berlin, 1819–21):

'Der Artushof' ('The Artushof', 1819), trans. in *Tales*
'Die Automate' ('The Automata', 1819), trans. in Bleiler
'Die Bergwerke zu Falun' ('The Mines at Falun', 1819), trans. in Bleiler, *Tales* and Zipes
'Doge und Dogaresse' ('The Doge and His Wife', 1819), trans. in *Tales*
'Die Fermate' ('The Fermata', 1819)
'Das fremde Kind' ('The Strange Child' 1819), trans. in Bell and (as 'The Mystifying Child') Zipes
'Der Kampf der Sänger' ('The Singers' Contest', 1818)
'Nussknacker und Mausekönig' ('The Nutcracker and the Mouse-King', 1819), trans. in Bleiler, Bell and Zipes
'Rat Krespel' ('Krespel the Councillor', 1819), trans. in Bleiler and *Tales*
'Die Brautwahl' ('The Choosing of the Bride', 1820), trans. in *Tales*
'Das Fräulein von Scuderi' ('Mademoiselle de Scudery', 1820), trans. in *Tales*

Stories not Collected in Hoffmann's Lifetime

Prinzessin Brambilla (Princess Brambilla, 1821), trans. in GP
Meister Floh (Master Flea, published in censored form 1822, in uncensored form 1908), trans. in GP
'Des Vetters Eckfenster' ('My Cousin's Corner Window', 1822), trans. in GP

Novels

Die Elixiere des Teufels, 2 vols (Berlin, 1815–16), trans. Ronald Taylor as *The Devil's Elixirs* (London, 1963, repr. 2008, reissued 2017)
Lebens-Ansichten des Katers Murr, 2 vols (Berlin, 1819–21), trans. Anthea Bell as *The Life and Opinions of the Tomcat Murr* (London, 1999)

Essays and Dialogues

'Beethovens Instrumental-Musik' ('Beethoven's Instrumental Music', 1813), in *Fantasiestücke*; trans. in C
'Der Dichter und der Komponist' ('The Poet and the Composer', 1813), in *Die Serapions-Brüder*; trans. in C
'Alte und neue Kirchenmusik' ('Old and New Church Music', 1814), trans. in C
Seltsame Leiden eines Theater-Direktors (Strange Sufferings of a Theatre Director, 1819)

Miscellaneous Prose Works

'Drei verhängnisvolle Monate!' ('Three Fateful Months!', 1813)
'Der Dey von Elba in Paris' ('The Dey of Elba in Paris', 1814)
'Die Vision auf dem Schlachtfelde von Dresden' ('The Vision on the Battlefield of Dresden', 1814)

Musical Works

Die Maske (The Mask), *Singspiel*, 1799, text by Hoffmann
Scherz, List und Rache (Jest, Cunning and Revenge), *Singspiel*, 1801, text by Johan Wolfgang von Goethe
Die lustigen Musikanten (The Merry Musicians), *Singspiel*, 1804, text by Clemens Brentano
Der Renegat (The Renegade), opera fragment, 1804
Dirna, opera, 1809, text by Count Julius von Soden
Miserere in B-flat minor, 1809
Aurora, opera, 1812, text by Franz von Holbein
Undine, opera, 1816, text by Friedrich de la Motte Fouqué

Select Commentary on Hoffmann in English

Brown, Hilda Meldrum, *E.T.A. Hoffmann and the Serapiontic Principle: Critique and Creativity* (Rochester, NY, 2006)

Daemmrich, Horst S., *The Shattered Self: E.T.A. Hoffmann's Tragic Vision* (Detroit, MI, 1973)

Dutchman-Smith, Victoria, *E.T.A. Hoffmann and Alcohol: Biography, Reception and Art* (Leeds, 2020)

Ellis, John M., 'E.T.A. Hoffmann's *Das Fräulein von Scuderi*', *Modern Language Review*, LXIV/2 (1969), pp. 340–50

—, 'Hoffmann: *Rat Krespel*', in *Narration in the German Novelle* (Cambridge, 1974), pp. 94–112

—, 'Clara, Nathanael, and the Narrator: Interpreting Hoffmann's *Der Sandmann*', *German Quarterly*, LIV/1 (1981), pp. 1–18

Hewett-Thayer, H. W., *Hoffmann: Author of the Tales* (Princeton, NJ, 1948)

Murnane, Barry, 'Fantastic Histories and Discursive Doubles: Scott, Hoffmann, Alexis and De Quincey', *Angermion*, IX/1 (2016), pp. 1–43

Negus, Kenneth, *E.T.A. Hoffmann's Other World: The Romantic Author and His 'New Mythology'* (Philadelphia, PA, 1965)

Neilly, Joanna, *E.T.A. Hoffmann's Orient: Romantic Aesthetics and the German Imagination* (Cambridge, 2016)

Prawer, S. S., 'Hoffmann's Uncanny Guest: A Reading of *Der Sandmann*', *German Life and Letters*, XVIII/4 (1965), pp. 297–308

Reddick, John, 'E.T.A. Hoffmann's *Der Goldne Topf* and Its "Durchgehaltene Ironie"', *Modern Language Review*, LXXI/3 (1976), pp. 577–94

Riou, Jeanne, 'Music and Non-Verbal Reason in E.T.A. Hoffmann', in *Music and Literature in German Romanticism*, ed. Siobhán Donovan and Robin Elliott (Rochester, NY, 2004), pp. 43–55

Robertson, Ritchie, 'Shakespearean Comedy and Romantic Psychology in Hoffmann's *Kater Murr*', *Studies in Romanticism*, XXIV/2 (1985), pp. 201–22

—, '"Unerforschliches Verhängnis!" The Vocabulary of "Fate" in E.T.A. Hoffmann's *Die Elixiere des Teufels*', *Studi Germanici*, 25 (2024), pp. 69–92

Röder, Birgit, *A Study of the Major Novellas of E.T.A. Hoffmann* (Rochester, NY, 2003)

Schafer, R. Murray, *E.T.A. Hoffmann and Music* (Toronto, 1975)

Taylor, Ronald, *Hoffmann* (Cambridge, 1963)

Wright, Elizabeth, *E.T.A. Hoffmann and the Rhetoric of Terror* (London, 1978)

Zilcosky, John, 'Hoffmann at the Battle of Dresden: "The Sandman" and the Napoleonic Wars', in *The Language of Trauma: War and Technology in Hoffmann, Freud, and Kafka* (Toronto, 2021), pp. 17–40

Zipes, Jack, 'Introduction: E.T.A. Hoffmann, the Wounded Storyteller', in *The Wounded Storyteller: The Traumatic Tales of E.T.A. Hoffmann*, trans. Jack Zipes (New Haven, CT, 2023), pp. xiv–xxiii

Acknowledgements

A great deal of information about Hoffmann's life can be gathered from his letters, his diaries and the recollections of friends and acquaintances. The last were collected and edited by the indefatigable Hoffmann scholar Friedrich Schnapp in a volume entitled *Aufzeichnungen* (see Abbreviations and Citations). The indispensable edition of Hoffmann's writings is the one edited by Hartmut Steinecke et al., likewise listed there. Steinecke also wrote what I would call the best study of Hoffmann, with subtle interpretations of all his literary works: *Die Kunst der Fantasie: E.T.A. Hoffmanns Leben und Werk* (2004).

In writing this book I have received invaluable help from two friends, the Hoffmann scholar Joanna Neilly and the Beethoven expert Laura Tunbridge. Laura saved me from some blunders concerning Hoffmann and music and brought me up to date with the relevant research. I thank them both warmly. Any remaining mistakes are entirely my own.

Photo Acknowledgements

The author and publishers wish to express their thanks to the sources listed below for illustrative material and/or permission to reproduce it. Some locations of works are also given below, in the interest of brevity:

Art Institute of Chicago: pp. 50, 111; imfotograf/AdobeStock: p. 97; Kupferstichkabinett, Staatliche Museen zu Berlin: pp. 12 (Jörg P. Anders), 21 and 74 (Volker-H. Schneider), 103 (Jörg P. Anders), 124 (Volker-H. Schneider); from Charles Lafontaine, *L'art de magnétiser ou le magnétisme animal* (Paris, 1847), photo Wellcome Collection, London: p. 45; from Friedrich de la Motte-Fouqué, *Undine*, trans. W. L. Courtney (London and New York, 1909), photo Information and Library Science Library, University of North Carolina at Chapel Hill: p. 105; Nationalgalerie, Staatliche Museen zu Berlin/Jörg P. Anders: p. 100; Staatsbibliothek Bamberg (CC BY-SA 4.0): pp. 35 (V A 227), 37 (Nc.f.141), 40 (OFS.G H 2), 42 (I T 80), 44 (V A 225c), 59 (Nc.f.141), 90 (Sel.281), 108 (EvS.G H 2/1), 118 and 119 (Sel.229), 128 (Autogr. H 31); Staatsbibliothek zu Berlin: pp. 65, 73 (photo bpk/Rudolf Albert Schwarz); Stadtmuseum Berlin, photo akg-images: p. 76; from *Le Théâtre*, XV/325 (1 July 1912): p. 83; photo Tilman2007/Wikimedia Commons (CC BY-SA 4.0): p. 32; Yale Center for British Art, New Haven, CT: p. 53.